Federico Fellini

edited by Lietta Tornabuoni

RIZZOLI
NEW YORK

First published in the United States of America in 1995 by
RIZZOLI INTERNATIONAL PUBLICATIONS, INC.
300 Park Avenue South, New York, NY 10010

The original Italian language edition was published
to coincide with the Federico Fellini exhibition at
Palazzo della Civiltà, Salone delle Fontane, in Rome
20 January 1995 - 26 March 1995

ISBN 0-8478-1878-0
LC 95-68131

Designed by Studio Massa & Marti
English language translation by Andrew Ellis, Carol Rathman, David Stanton

Printed and bound in Italy

Acknowledgments

Special thanks to
the heirs of Federico Fellini
and Giulietta Masina

and also to
Pier Luigi Bersani
Felicia Bottino
Gianni Borgna
Giuseppe Chicchi
Franco Lucchesi
Giacomo Miceli
Vittorio Novelli
Carmelo Rocca
Francesco Rutelli

Giovanni Arnone
Elisabetta Bruscolini
Silvano Cibò
Francesco Gencarelli
Giuseppe Gherpelli
Gianfranco Miro Gori
Roberto Grandi
Andrea Jengo
Ennio Longardi
Giulia Mafai
Raffaele Maiello
Ermanno Neri
Davide Rampello
Maurizio Sartori
Flavia Schiavi
Pasquale Squitieri
Bruno Torri
Carlo Troilo
Maurizio Venafro
Marcello Visconti

Gianfranco Angelucci
Liliana Betti
Maria Celo Pessione (for the Fabrizi archives)
Enzo De Castro
Stefano dello Schiavo
Raffaella Donato
Dante Ferretti
Paolo Ferrari
Giuliano Geleng
Norma Giacchero
Galleria Vittoria
Tullio Kezich
Maurizio Mein
Ibrahim Moussa
Mauro Paganelli
Carlo Patrizi
Alex Ponti
Renzo Rossellini
Leopoldo Trieste
Nino Za
Germana Zanini

Giuseppe De Luca
Hotel Excelsior, Gran Caffè Doney,
and other hotels in Rome
Regina Baglioni, Majestic, Eden, Jolly.
Anna Mode 68
Mariella Porta

Lenders
Giulio Andreotti
Gideon Bachmann
Daniela Barbiani
Britta Barnes
Daniela Barnes
Michele Barnes
Anna Maria Bassetti
Franca Bassetti
Liliana Betti
Biblioteca Gambalunga
Biblioteca Nerbini
Maurizio Baroni
Giuseppe Bruno Bossio
Cam
Alessandro Carletti
Massimo Caruana
Cinecittà
Giorgio Conti (Archivio della Modernità)
Pier Marco De Santi
Eredi De Santis
Eredi Fabrizi
Comune di Reggiolo
Comune di Rimini
Osvaldo De Micheli
Enrico De Seta
Maurizio Dell'Amore
Jolanda Di Pasquale
Ente Cinema
Vincenzo Fazio
Massimo Davanzati
Galleria Mascherino
Antonello Geleng
Giuliano Geleng
Rinaldo Geleng
Rita Giacchero
Armando Giuffrida
GP 11 Srl
Daniel Keel-Diogenes Verlag
Lilly Library of Rare Books - Indiana University
Leda Lojodice
Ennio Longardi
Mario Longardi
Milo Manara
Roberto Mannoni
Maurizio Mein
Melanton
Marcella Menaglia
Vincenzo Mollica
Aldo Nemni
Alessandro Nicosia
Pietro Notarianni
Domenico Pertica
Fiammetta Profili
Silvio Pozzi
Gian Luigi Rondi
Sandro Simeoni
Grazyna Sitkiewicz
Giovannangelo Tavanti
Videa S.p.A.
Germana Zanini

Production and distribution
Academy
Aljiosha Productions
Cinecittà
Cecchi Gori Group
Cristaldi Film
Dino De Laurentiis Communication
Gaumont
Istituto Luce
Leone Cinematografica
Mediaset Srl
Mondadori Video
New Pentax Film
Paradise Film
PEA Film
RAI (Radio Televisione Italiana)
RCS Films
Renzo Rossellini
Rete Italia
Titanus
Vides Cinematografica
Warner Bros

Graphic designers
Luigi De Santis
Enrico De Seta
Rinaldo Geleng
Giuliano Geleng
Mauro Innocenti
Milo Manara
Giorgio Olivetti
Andrea Pazienza
Luigi Rovere
Sandro Simeoni

Photographers
Nicola Arresto
Rosario Assenza
Gideon Bachmann
Deborah Beer
Tiziana Callari
Elisabetta Catalano
Minno Cattarinich/Ram Studio
Osvaldo Civirani
Pietro Coccia/Granata Press Service
Emilio Lari
Franco Pinna
G.B. Poletto
Pierluigi Praturlon/Reporters Associati
Paul Ronald/AFE
Enrica Scalfari/AGF
Tazio Secchiaroli

Contents

Foreword by Martin Scorsese
Preface by Lietta Tornabuoni

For quite a while I had been wanting to introduce my younger daughter, now seventeen, to the cinema of Federico Fellini and the obvious place to start seemed to be *La Strada*. After all, here was a "vintage Fellini": the circus and the seashore, piazzas at night and open-air weddings, humor and compassion in a world that is often hostile and grotesque, yet magical and full of apparitions, of surprise, where laughter and melancholy are intermingled. Also there are Nino Rota's musical score, Otello Martelli's black-and-white photography and, most of all, Giulietta Masina's memorable performance as Gelsomina, the simple-minded waif dominated by a brutal strongman.

As the movie unfolded, I realized that I hadn't quite prepared my daughter for its emotional impact and its mesmerizing power. Nearly forty years after the film was made, the parable of redemption hidden beneath an apparently picaresque plot had become even more compelling and lyrical.

I remember wher I first saw *La Strada*. I was about twelve, and I accepted the film at face value. But I heard my parents discuss it with relatives, and I specifically remember their complaints about the English dubbing. I guess they meant that the language was essential to the magic realism of the movie.

Later, when I studied the film, I found myself particularly fascinated by The Fool (played by Richard Basehart). His teasing of the strongman, Zampanò (Anthony Quinn), finally goes one step too far—which seals his fate. I was captivated by the building of tension between the two, by the clash of conflicting spirits traveling the same road but on separate quests. I also found myself attracted to Zampanò and the dark side of human nature that he reveals—something I later explored in my own films. I was enthralled by the film's resolution, where the power of the spirit overwhelms brute force.

La Strada had been preceded by *Variety Lights* (which Fellini co-directed with Alberto Lattuada, in 1950), *The White Sheik* (1952) and *I Vitelloni* (1953)—another Fellini picture with a pivotal influence on my work. His highly personal vision, expressed in a lyrical and imaginative style, was a major break from the neorealist films of postwar Italy—

mainly Roberto Rossellini's *Open City* and *Paisan*, Vittorio De Sica's *Shoeshine*, *Bicycle Thief* and *Umberto D*, and Luchino Visconti's *Terra Trema*.

Neorealism was a moment in world cinema born of historical circumstances (the disastrous conditions of postwar Italy and the limited means of film production), and it became (mostly thanks to Rossellini) a specific style of film making, characterized by the use of real locations, nonprofessional actors, an almost documentary approach to contemporary stories, and much technical ingenuity. By the early 1950s neorealism had become a noun, codified and limited in scope, if not in style. Most of all, Marxist critics had politicized it.

By contrast, Fellini's autobiographical, spiritual, and magical world did not fit easily into an ideology or code. He was continuously rediscovering the cinema, reinventing it, exploring its unique properties, which set film apart from any other art.

What Fellini carried over from neorealism into his films was what one might call an overwhelming sense of the physical world. His images are always concrete, almost tangible, even when they're at their most fantastic. André Bazin, the great French film critic, also pointed out the Franciscan side of neorealism—a basic, direct approach to truth and faith that is present in *La Strada*.

This physicality, this immediacy, miraculously eliminates the imaginary space between film and spectator. It draws you in. As the Italian author Italo Calvino said about Fellini:

"The cinema of distance which nourished our youth is turned forever on its head in the cinema of absolute proximity. For the brief span of our lifetimes, everything remains there on the screen, distressingly present; first images of eros and premonitions of death catch up with us in every dream; the end of the world began with us and shows no signs of ending; the film we thought we were merely watching is the story of our lives."

Martin Scorsese

Martin Scorsese
Copyright © 1993 by The New York Times Company. Reprinted by permission.

"You mustn't understand. Woe betide you if you understand. You must just listen, just hear...." Federico Fellini said that these words, pronounced by the moon-woman in his last film, *The Voice of the Moon*, were both the expression and summary of the only aesthetic ideals that were possible for him: his willingness to accept both reality and unreality, the spirit with which he was ready to welcome everything in the world, a natural lack of judgmental or rationalizing attitudes. Perhaps it was true, perhaps not: but this was what the great artist, the imaginative genius, the superb storyteller, the giant of the cinema, loved to think about himself (or wanted others to think about him) when he was seventy years old. Now, as the twentieth century draws to a close, this commemoration of Fellini does not only involve remembering the film-maker who has enriched the imaginations of millions of individuals, or recalling episodes from the life—the legend, very often—of a man who has represented, influenced, and, at times, conditioned, western culture in the second half of this century. Thus, it must not be a celebration of the man, but it should also be an opportunity to obtain a more profound knowledge and a real understanding of how Fellini worked and lived.

The international exhibition, for which this book is the decidedly unusual catalogue, is the first attempt to make a detailed appraisal of Fellini's universe after the death of the great director. More specifically, this volume aims to provide, apart from the biography and filmography, a portrait of Federico Fellini in his less-well known aspects, using material that is either unpublished, or that was published long ago, or is obscure, or has simply been forgotten.

Four hitherto unpublished texts describe films that Fellini never made. Their subject-matter is as follows: the nature and psychology of the actor; Venice, the ethereal, magic city on water; the director bewildered by the never-ending entreaties from producers, especially American and Japanese, that he should direct a film based on the *Inferno* in Dante's *Divine Comedy*; Mandrake, the hero of the illusion, the adventurous elegance, and the sheer enchantment of the American comic strips of the thirties that so fascinated the director. Fellini's unpublished correspondence with other film-makers, artists, and famous writers are evidence of his relationship with internationally famous personalities who were socially his peers, yet were very different as human beings. Whether they express his thoughts with regard to censorship and political commitment, or reflect his moods, light-hearted or dispirited, these letters are all written in a straightforward style, unadorned by reverential turns of phrase when addressing the mighty. Fellini's descriptions of his dreams, accompanied by splendid drawings, allow us to glimpse at least a part of the oneiric world that had such a major influence on the creation of his films.

The examples of the way Fellini meticulously contributed to the realization of comic strips of the films that he never made—they include written instructions and are drawn so precisely that they constitute a form of direction—are the most poignant reminders of the extent to which he missed the cinema in the last years of his life, when he was obliged, against his will, to be inactive.

Unpublished or little-known drawings and photographs complete this research, which has been made more complex by Fellini's unique personality. In fact, the great director's special traits were evident in his working methods, which were often very confusing for others. In the second half of his life, Fellini tended to destroy letters, notes, and documents, joking that he suffered from the "murderer's syndrome" that induced him to eliminate everything that might possibly be incriminating evidence, or even merely be proof of his presence or existence. In his cinema, on the other hand, the opposite propensity for keeping everything may be found. This is particularly evident in the images relating to his childhood or adolescence; unlike this day and age, it was a period when the image could have an absolute, everlasting value. A childhood image—a person bound to a railroad track, a train approaching inexorably—was linked, according to Fellini, to his initial discovery of the theater, although it was common at the time in westerns or illustrations of adventure stories. It appears again in dreams that he illustrated in 1974, in *The Voice of the Moon* (1990), where the train becomes a woman-steam locomotive, and in a television commercial he made in 1992.

Another of Fellini's tendencies was that of never attributing (not openly, anyhow) any value to authenticity or the chronology of his work as a scenarist, scriptwriter, and draftsman. He thought nothing of changing dates, antedating or postdating drawings if this was useful at the time; he manipulated, cancelled, and remade; he claimed authorship of texts that he had commissioned others to write; he used old texts in new contexts; he moved blocks of narrative or characters from one version to the other of the same text, or from one text to another; at times he incorporated the writings of others into his own work; and he poked fun at those who were scandalized by such effrontery. He used his material in the same way that artists, whether they be writers, painters, or anything else, have always done. As a result, however, any attribution or dating of his works apart from his films is necessarily open to question.

Maybe he was right. In the course of time, it seems that Fellini as a celebrity, and the world that surrounded him, overwhelmed Fellini as a film director: but it is his films, his way of creating cinema, that have remained unique and unforgettable.

Lietta Tornabuoni

Originally a journalist, Fellini made his first foray into the world of film in 1942, writing scripts, gags, screenplays, and dialogues; throughout his career he continued to write books, to write screenplays for his films in conjunction with others, and to sketch out new ideas for possible future films.

The texts published here—just part of numerous unpublished writings found among Fellini's archives—illustrate a virtual side to Fellini's film output, his dream world, his hopes, together with creations or ideas that never made it to celluloid for a variety of reasons, such as lack of funds, sudden loss of interest, shift of focus to some other project, or the director's illness or death. These writings encompass short stories, synopses, jottings, sketches of shots, and proposals of all kinds. Here we find pages of ideas, some finished and intriguing, story-lines that make us regret that he never actually managed to set them to film, ideas that give us insights into the desires and curiosity of their author. Such secret writings reveal Fellini's ability as an author: his work brims with ideas and surprises, with humor and memories.

Published here for the first time, these works are an essential part of the Fellini legacy. Written over a period of twenty years (1972–92), occasionally in association with a co-writer, they were registered with the Italian authors' and writers' guild to safeguard the copyright, and are published here in reverse order: from his last writings to those of less recent date. The texts are complemented with the notes, sketches and jottings Fellini made on his dreams (a practice he adopted from 1960 onward), all gathered in bound volumes entitled "Libri dei sogni" (Books of Dreams). These writings are accompanied by hitherto unpublished material from his comic books of ideas, which he sketched out ready for transfer to full drawings, or for the big screen itself. As a result, this anthology gives a well-rounded picture of the man: Fellini the writer and artist, Fellini the dreamer.

The Actor or *Actor* is the last concrete project that Fellini worked on, from 1992 until the spring of 1993. It was to be one of the televised specials included in a contract with RAI (Radiotelevisione Italiana), for the series *Block-notes di un regista* (A Director's Notebook); other possible installments of the series were *Venice*, *Naples*, *Inferno*, and two stories about why, despite numerous requests, Fellini had never shot a film in the United States nor staged an opera. The only one of these projects to reach an advanced stage of preparation was *The Actor*, a meditation on the craft and the particular psychology of the actor, conceived in the colloquial tones of a conversation through images, produced in Cinecittà by Leo Pescarolo with RAI and French partners. Initially written in a choral key, with many actors, its next phase concentrated on a single protagonist, Paolo Villaggio; it was always nourished by autobiographical elements (the discovery of theater and its protagonists, the melancholy of old age).

The following unpublished texts reflect the birth, modification, formation of the work: an initial idea; a broader, narrated treatment; scripted sequences; notes on themes, settings, characters; materials for a second version.

I would like to dedicate these Block Notes to the Actor, to this unique creature poised between reality and fiction, to the man-mask and his playful madness, and also to his defects, his vanity, his neurotic side, his psychology—at times childlike and a little bit schizoid. Alongside the Actor, I would like to talk about the appointed place where the actor acts, that complex of magic spaces that is a theater; the classical late-nineteenth-century Italian theater: over here, the stage, the backstage, the dressing rooms, foyers; over there, the tiers of shimmering gilt boxes, the gallery, the velvet orchestra seats, the colossal chandelier with its thousands of crystal drops which, when the performance is over, is slowly drawn up beyond the ceiling, disappearing beneath the roof in its enormous attic loft, dark and dusty.

Film notes shot in a single setting, in itself mysterious and evocative, a play of mirrors into which I would like to entice Mastroianni, Villaggio, Benigni, Gassman, and also Scaccia and Giulietta Masina. A grotesque, cheerful pastiche, like a carnival masquerade, a scarcely formal interweave of little stories, anecdotes, episodes, recollections, that leaves no room for smug analyses, psychologism, thoughtful seriousness, but which unfolds gracefully, lightly, a little bit inebriated and a little elusive, just like the nature of the Actor—exactly, elusive.

I note here the subjects, the situations, the roles that I envision for each character, without suggesting a succession, a construction, or how they will fit together; all this will take shape and vigor from the very flow of the images, from the alchemy of the attitudes, the feelings, emotions, from the very tone of voice with which the various passages of the story will be alternately whispered, prompted, proclaimed, confided.

I would like the chat to begin with Marcello (Mastroianni) who, on a rainy night, arrives in a taxi on the small central square of an unknown town. The taxi drives away and he, on the shiny cobblestones, sets out uncertainly, vaguely surprised and disoriented, toward a construction at the end of the square. It could be the town hall, the school, the train station. But instead it is the theater. But it is closed and deserted: sleeping. Through the grill of the shutter Marcello peers into the lobby just barely lit by the light from a streetlamp; the box office is empty, the doors closed, the lights turned off, the curtains drawn, the velvet seats in a neat row along the stuccoed walls.

In the classic little nineteenth-century theater, like so many others in every Italian town, there is not a living soul, no caretaker, no usher, nobody. Walking around the building, Marcello finally finds a little door left slightly ajar and he slips inside. But even inside the theater seems abandoned; there is nothing to suggest a rehearsal, a meeting, a show being mounted. Forging on, he chances on a series of passages and narrow corridors and finally emerges in the orchestra, silent and deserted: a vast white cloth covers the velvet seats like a great stormy sea or a field cloaked in snow. The boxes are empty and dark and the chandelier up there, in the center of the ceiling, is halfway in its attic loft. No noise, apart from the gurgling of the water in the pipes and the patter of the rain on the roof.

The actor moves instinctively toward the stage, walks around it, disappears in the thickest shadow, and after a while, reappears on the proscenium, barely illuminated by a feeble service light who knows where. "But Federico, what have you got me into?" he complains, demoralized. "There's nobody! It's cold in here and I haven't even eaten ..." I would try to ask him if he wants something to eat, but I am sure that Marcello would immediately answer, "No, to eat, no. Maybe something to drink, if I could have a little glass …. You know, when I have to do something, it helps a little, a drop'll pick you up …." Then I would like Marcello, cheered by the alcohol, inspired by the suggestiveness of the place, to begin a little at a time to settle into his role, to recount, perhaps remembering his first encounter with actors. And to talk about that morning when, as a child, behind the garden of his house he suddenly heard the unfurling with a rumble of the great roller-shutter of the adjacent building (the Politeama Theater) and inside spied a man and a woman sitting in the shadows, he with a beret and overcoat, she with her knitting: they are running through their lines in a dialogue about a forced-open window and a certain Sergeant Jonathan. They were two actors from the Bella–Starace–Sainati company who were rehearsing a *Grand Guignol*.

Helped up by the man's hands, the boy enters the dark theater and sees the gilt boxes all around him and, over his head, looming, suspended, fluttering between red, white, and yellow celluloids, the belly of a locomotive. That same evening or the one after, the boy, now dressed in a little sailor's suit, would see the same, awesome locomotive advancing threateningly amidst whistles, screeches, and headlights that grow bigger and bigger as they draw nearer to the woman lashed to the tracks …. The actress is saved at the last minute by the hero, and an enormous, heavy, soft red curtain falls on her. It was the theater. A scene, a curtain, and an inebriating labyrinth of orchestra seats, velvet, brass, trimmings, hallways, mysterious passageways, through which the child had scampered like a mouse during intermission. The emotion had been so strong that it did not abandon him for the entire night.

Now, I want Marcello to talk about all this, and about the actors who, like semidivine creatures, appear one morning on the road to school, surfacing from the fog, in the photographs past-

ed to the wall, signed across the bottom with a flourish: Majeroni, Febo Mari, Gustavo Giorgi, Benassi, Moissi. These were the names that accompanied stern expressions, flashing eyes, bitter smiles, imperious profiles, and long, flowing hair, sometimes nearly reaching to the shoulders, like Majeroni's in *Ghosts*.

These regal and romantic countenances appeared suddenly in the winter, usually just before Carnival, on the house fronts, in the windows of the Caffè Commercio, on the square, at the station, and from up there gazed down like deities beyond our reach, promising that they might just come one day, just maybe, that they would have materialized. They were thought to be supernatural beings, another race, and the Albergo Leon D'Oro which accommodated them for a few nights took on the mythical proportions of Olympus. It was difficult to imagine what an actor's life could be offstage or off the white movie screen. "Majeroni, though," Marcello relates, "I had had the luck to see him, standing erect at the counter of the Dovesi pastry shop, with a long, white silk scarf, a pearl-gray Homburg on his head, a faint trace of makeup: he sipped through a straw something that was steaming hot in a small glass with a silver handle. Mandarin punch, the waiter told us later."

Marcello should also talk of the solitude of the stage, when the actor is alone with his character and before him is the indistinct public, a dark, breathing mass, lying in ambush, so close, yet so far, remote, invisible. Somewhere out there, there must be a friend, but where is he? And he should mention the problem of memory, the sudden blanks, that terrifying specter, the certainty of remembering everything and then … like in nightmares, when you have to run and your legs won't move.

And finally, he should linger over old age. When he leaves his bedroom ever so quietly and closes the door, waiting a few minutes in the hall, then abruptly opens it and sticks his head in, sniffing deeply to see if the room where he slept smells of old age.

He says that it's not true that old age creeps up on you, but instead it comes suddenly, from one day to the next. He is sitting in the corner of a railway car and since it is night outside, the window reflects his face. There is somebody else with him in the compartment, somebody who does not look at all like him, a completely different person. They exchange a few lines of dialogue: can that person be him? "But how did it happen? How can I have changed so much?" asks Marcello. "You've never said anything to me, not so much as a hint, a sign, an early warning, I've been going on trusting you, as ever. How many years do I still have to live?"

The train is slowing down and he makes a decision; but yes, he gets off and lets the old man continue on his way. From the platform he watches the train pull away. But it is the old man who got off; Marcello stayed on the train that is taking him who knows where. The nameless old man remains alone in the deserted and unknown little station.

There, along with Marcello, in a play of citations, references, associations, I see all the others, like a sort of elect lineup of the art of performance and mime, of the theatrical and cinematographic memory.

Paolo Villaggio would be perfect in the glorious role of Jiggs, together with Giulietta Masina, who would play Maggie. With them, I would like to revive McManus's classic comic strip: Maggie, at the piano, wants to sing Schubert and her husband in gaiters and string tie tries to make his escape through the window, to go and eat fish and chips with his bricklayer friends. Naturally, it all concludes with a blow on the head with Maggie's rolling pin and a duet sung by the two actors.

But first, as he prepares to transform himself into the cartoon character, Villaggio, too, will have talked about actors: what distinguishes an actor from a non-actor, who can be said to have an actor's face? He could also make a little disquisition on his own face, which he does not consider an actor's face.

Giulietta, too, should talk about this aspect as well as about the natural inclinations of actors, who are sometimes forced to play roles that are not suited to them or about which they do not agree with the director. Masina claims that her roles would be romantic ones, completely different from the ones that she is usually required to perform. She would like to do heroines' parts, where they wear beautiful costumes, in touching love stories with scenes and musical themes that move you to tears. Thus, I can see Giulietta telling in a comic way of the tense, quarrelsome, and sometimes even violent relationships that can arise between actor and director. Widely divergent approaches to a part, ways of perceiving a character, and then the disputes, rifts, insults, threats of abandonment, the anger, the humiliation, the actress's demands that the director act out for her the female role, mocking him in front of everybody ....

At one time, at least, there were the genres that kept things straight. The actors were distinguished by character types: comic actors and comedians, dramatic and light actors, foils, leading lovers, character actors, fine narrators. Each role had its precise qualities. Each had its look: Benassi, Febo Mari, Ninchi, Ruggeri. And Zacconi.

Villaggio could tell about the first time he saw Ermete Zacconi, as a child, he, too, dressed in a little sailor's suit, during a summer vacation at Santa Margherita Ligure. The great tragic actor was performing in *La Morte Civile*, his calling card, but by then truly aged, he could no longer withstand the fatigue of the entire show. So he did not come onstage until the final scene, when he performed the death by strychnine poisoning .... Villaggio himself (or Mario Scaccia) should here launch into this performance, doing all the spasms, shudders, writhing, while the audience implores enough already! get it over with, somebody do something, help him! But by now the iciness has gone beyond the level of the heart, and kicking like a dying animal, the actor gives up the ghost. Applause, tears, sobs, praise. The actor's apotheosis.

And here who else could come onto the scene but Vittorio Gassman, to describe this more than elating, inebriating, orgasmic moment that the actor experiences on the stage?

However, not before Villaggio has given us a taste of his twisted histrionics with an interpretation of a great, troubling character in the actor's universe, Professor Unrat, from the famous film (*The Blue Angel*) by Joseph von Sternberg, with Marlene Dietrich. His Blue Angel, though, comes in the shape of a very beautiful Brazilian transvestite, with such hypertrophic curves and proportions that they become unreal, oneiric, visionary. In a monstrous, delirious snarl of thighs, tits, tangas, transparent chiffons, loincloths, fishnet stockings, stiletto heels, plumed hats that not even Carmen Miranda or the most ostentatious of variety girls would have dared to wear, Villaggio takes one of these infernal dream creatures aboard his car.

Sinking ever deeper into an asphyxiating excitement, and despite a blinding desire, he cannot refrain from moralizing: he proclaims cultural alibis, makes a show of indignantly disapproving that trade in flesh, that social horror that leads to the exploitation of human weaknesses, of desperate youths who use bizarre aberrations and questionable inclinations to escape a destiny of misery and alienation from which nobody would help them get free. Thus, they are forced to prostitute themselves, to expose themselves in the most indecent, most obscene, most provocative ways, worse than the worst whores, giving themselves up to the first who comes along ....

Villaggio-Unrat blathers on and flounders about in his own reasoning, overcome by his arousal, fondling the monument of flesh that he has by his side, until finally he caves in all at once: "Yeeeess," he cries, no longer able to restrain himself, "do with me what you want, I'm yours, yours!"

Applause, standing ovations, never-ending clapping. This is an overwhelming chapter: the actor and gratitude. Gratitude is no small part of the dramatic art; to the contrary, it is communion with the public, it is the mystical flesh of the celebration, the deep emotion, the most intimate, morbid discomposure that sets in with the spectators' emotional response. On the one hand, the gratitude of the public, and on the other, the gratitude of the actor, his self-immolation, his delivering up of himself to that voracious, exclusive love that the public lavishes on him, in the end drowning him, swallowing him up.

The supreme artist of gratitude, says Gassman, the quintessence of this art within an art, was Salvo Randone. And it should be added: Randone in the final scene of *Henry IV* .... Only Gassman can come close to the mixture of ecstasy, transport, obnubilation, state of grace and suffering that long colored the face, with a heartrending effect, of the inimitable Randone when he came back for the curtain call to collect the tribute of applause, cries of Bravo! and Evviva! And only Gassman can conjure up and come close to the concert of strong emotions, studied to wring out the most delirious ovation. Death scenes are the most moving of all, the kind that put a knot in the throat of the public, dragging it from gasp after gasp, tremor after tremor, toward abysses of torment and uncontrollable tears. Ruggeri, Ricci, Benassi, each had his own rendering of death, masterful deaths, minutely studied, well before the Actors Studio, with long visits to hospital wards and chronic disease hospitals, really in touch with the dying. Anything for the public, for applause!

The two famous characters from the American comic strip by George McManus, singing in octosyllabic verses (in Italian) to the accompaniment of a charleston, recount a classic story about their marriage. The scenes, the places where the story takes place, will be constructed on the stage, in the Art Nouveau and Art Deco styles of the famous illustrator.

Scene 1

The vast living room of the house where the two characters live: an imposing staircase leading to the upper floors, sofas and armchairs in the above-mentioned styles, a grand piano, and in the background an open window covered by a voile curtain.

In this room, Maggie peremptorily orders Jiggs (who, in undershirt and dangling suspenders, is shuffling around the house in his slippers waiting for a chance to steal away) to go and get dressed for the musical afternoon where various members of the aristocracy will be present, as well as a famous musician who has graciously agreed to accompany Maggie on the piano while she sings a number of ballads. Jiggs offers only weak resistance, while Maggie shouts at a butler to accompany him to his room.

Later, the guests arrive and are ceremoniously announced. Jiggs, now dressed up very smartly, wanders sulkily and lost among all the elegant ladies and the haughty gentlemen with big mustaches and monocles. The famous musician, with long sideburns and a halo of hair, sits at the piano, and Maggie begins to sing at the top of her voice. Meanwhile, Jiggs creeps up to the window, and, unseen, manages to climb out of it.

Scene 2

The facade of the house: up there, on the third floor, we can see Jiggs come out of the window and flatten himself against the wall, standing precariously on the cornice. It is a dangerous situation, but maybe Maggie's high notes are even more threatening. Luckily, almost at the same height, in front of the window of the neighboring apartment, there is some scaffolding on which there are men at work. Among these are a couple of bricklayers who are friends of Jiggs, and, while Maggie's piercing trills can be heard through the window of his apartment, the two pals place Jiggs in a large bucket hanging from a pulley and then carefully lower him to the ground.

Scene 3

Here he is safe and sound on the sidewalk, where he is joined almost immediately by his two bricklayer friends. Great rejoicing for the deliverance from danger. Jiggs wants to offer his friends a drink, and, singing together, they go off to their usual haunt.

Scene 4

Dinty Moore's Bar. In shirtsleeves, a cigar in his mouth, in the smoky atmosphere of the bar, surrounded by his cheerful friends who drink and sing as if they did not have a care in the world, Jiggs is rubbing chalk on the tip of his cue in preparation for the stroke that will bring him victory in a game of billiards. Just then Maggie appears at the door armed with her terrible rolling pin; she swings it in the air like a boomerang and throws it. As the rolling pin flies through the air it rotates and whistles, and it hits Jiggs's head with scientific precision.

"Dai mettiti i calzoni!"
disse aspra Petronilla.
"Sarà una sera da ricconi
con la gente che sfavilla.

Non mi fare sfigurare
canterò qualche canzone".
"Come farò a scappare?"
pensò Baldo col magone,

mentre senza resistenza
infilava il fraccone
misurando la pazienza
con il sogno del fugone.

Agghindati a puntino
duchi, conti e marchesi
in attesa di spuntino
parlottavano cortesi.

Le signore ben bardate
eran tutte cerimonie:
"Ma che bello, oh guardate"
tra l'olezzo di colonie.

Arcibaldo s'aggirava
sconsolato, fuori posto
"Ma che vita," brontolava
"molto fumo, ma l'arrosto?"

Il pianista basettone
ispirato e solenne
cominciò il concertone
con la chioccia senza penne.

Così era Petronilla
spietata canterina
ogni nota una scintilla
che spaccava la vetrina.

Stonato dagli acuti
Arcibaldo zitto, zitto
li lasciò senza saluti
scappando fuori dritto.

Si trovò sul cornicione
"Mamma mia, che paura"
barcollando d'emozione
di salvarsi lui scongiura.

"Io là dentro non ci torno"
e sperava nei pompieri,

"Come on, put on your pants!"
said Maggie very bitterly.
"It's a soirée for the upper crust
with lots of scintillating people.

Please don't give me a bad name,
a few songs I want to sing."
"How can I get out of this?"
thought Jiggs with grief,

as, without resistance,
he put his tails on,
trying not to lose his patience,
despite his great desire to flee.

Dressed up to the nines,
dukes, counts, and marquises,
waiting for the snack to begin,
talked so awfully politely.

The well-dressed ladies
were all standing on ceremony:
"Oh, how beautiful, oh do look,"
amidst the fragrance of cologne.

Jiggs wandered around,
disconsolate, out of place.
"What a life!" he grumbled,
"much ado about nothing!"

The pianist with sideburns,
inspired and solemn,
began the concert
with the featherless hen.

Thus was Maggie
a pitiless warbler,
and every note a blast
that broke the window.

Deafened by the high notes,
quietly Jiggs left them
without saying goodbye,
fleeing outside straightaway.

Now he was on the cornice:
"Good heavens, how scary!"
Swaying with fear,
imploring them to save him.

"I won't go back in there,"
he was hoping the firemen

per fortuna tutt'attorno
era pieno di cantieri.

Un amico muratore
nel vederlo vacillare
lanciò l'amo salvatore:
"Col secchio devi calare!"

Atterando Arcibaldo
grandi feste pregustava
con un fare da ribaldo
molti amici invitava.

Lui al solito ritrovo
Petronilla si scordava
si sentiva come nuovo
ed in coro poi cantava:

"Viva, viva la baldoria
che cancella i pensieri
siamo tutti senza gloria,
ma beviamo volentieri".

Attirato dal biliardo
ingessata la sua stecca
pensava già all'azzardo
senza fare mai cilecca.

Quando tutto si compiva
nel finale di partita
Petronilla appariva
ululando da tradita:

"Mascalzone, perdigiorno
mi fai sempre sfigurare,
ma io ora ti frastorno
non tentare di scappare".

E lanciando il matterello
lo colpisce sulla testa,
è un vecchio ritornello
alla fine della festa.

Arcibaldo rintronato
ascoltava gli uccellini
che con tempo ritmato
canticchiavan birichini:

"Viva, viva la baldoria
che cancella i pensieri
siamo tutti senza gloria,
ma beviamo volentieri".

would come. Luckily all around,
there was lots of scaffolding.

A bricklayer friend, seeing
him totter, launched
the saving hook: "You must
go down in the bucket!"

On landing, Jiggs
anticipated great celebrations,
and, roguishly, he invited
many of his friends.

At the usual haunt
Maggie was soon forgotten.
He felt like a new man
and in a chorus they sang:

"Long live fun and games
that help us forget our troubles.
We are all without glory,
but we drink willingly."

Tempted by the billiards,
having put chalk on his cue,
he was thinking of the game
in which he never failed.

Everything came to an end
with the final match.
Maggie suddenly appeared
yelling that she'd been betrayed:

"Scoundrel, idler: thanks to you
I always cut a poor figure,
but now I'll stun you.
don't try to run away."

And, throwing the rolling pin,
she hit him on the head;
it's a familiar refrain
after all the fun has ended.

Jiggs, dazed as he was,
listened to the birdies
that with a bright rhythm
sang mischievously:

"Long live fun and games
that help us forget our troubles.
We are all without glory,
but we drink willingly."

Federico Fellini

STORIE DI ATTORI

~~Immaginiamo che una giorno~~, Arrivano alla spicciolata,
uno dopo l'altro, e alcuni anche insieme, chiacchierando del
più e del meno, fumando la sigaretta, finendo di leggere il gior~~nale~~, qualcuno al bar si scotta col caffè bollente, ~~immaginia-
mo di scorgere tutte queste persone, che come in parte avete già
riconosciuto, appartengono al mondo dello spettacolo qualcuno
qualcosa quel o altri più o meno~~ *Sono attori, ne vi sono
dato apposatamente ne riconoscete qualcuno*
in un teatro e adesso ~~ricordiamone alcuni~~ (Mastroianni, ~~Buzzanca~~,
Pietro De Vico... Li vediamo
~~anne~~, la Masina, Paolo Villaggio) ~~li vediamo~~ salire sul palcoscenico deserto e prendere posto compostamente su delle sedie
sistemate senz'ordine qua e là.

Chi li ha convocati? Cosa sono venuti a fare alla
stessa ora su quel palcoscenico?

Guardandosi l'un l'altro con comica espressione di i-
gnoranza e indicando con insistenza l'orologio da polso come a
sottolineare la fretta, gli attori adesso seguono con gli occhi un personaggetto magro e scattante che passeggiando avanti
e indietro sembra riflettere se il modo in cui gli attori si
sono seduti è soddisfacente o no. In qualche caso deve parer-
gli che la sistemazione non va proprio bene; e allora batten-

They trickle in, one after the other, some in groups, chatting about this and that, smoking cigarettes, reading the rest of the newspaper, someone at the coffee bar burns himself drinking a scalding hot coffee. They are actors, they have arranged to meet at a theater and now you will recognize some of them (Mastroianni, Giulietta Masina, Paolo Villaggio, Pietro De Vico...). We see them enter the deserted stage and calmly take their places on the chairs set here and there in no particular arrangement.

Who called them here? What have they all come to do at the same time on that stage? Looking at one another with comical expressions of bewilderment and pointing insistently to their watches as if to show their impatience, the actors now follow with their eyes a thin, tense, small figure who, pacing back and forth, seems to be contemplating whether the order in which the actors have taken their places is suitable or not. In some cases, he must think that it certainly is not; so very lightly clapping his hands, he makes a nervous gesture inviting two or three to change places. Then, with his hands pressed together as if in prayer and measuring off the stage in long paces, risking a couple of times falling off it, the young man asks a rhetorical question out loud; and the vast deserted theater from the shadows sends back the echo several times: "The actor," intones the figure, "all right, but what is the actor? What is the *identikit* of the authentic psychological type that we call actor? What are the characteristics, the quirks that they share? What is the organic, biological drive that makes them become what they are?"

In the empty eye sockets of the boxes the echo of the words fades away. And an incredulous scepticism or an exaggerated show of attention now plays over the faces of the participants, and before so many questions

ironic little smiles start to beam, at the same time revealing just a trace of smugness.

At this point, we seem to gather from the little fellow's free-wheeling chatter, which he continues to spout, that this meeting has to do with a television program that would try to bring the continent-actor to the surface, to trace a possible map of the "territory-actor." And this would be done through their remarks, their vices, their childlike extroversion, their vanity, slightly neurotic sense of going beyond reality, ambition, egotistic delirium. And their little tales, stories, true or invented or imagined or altered by memory, anecdotes, fantasies, secrets, confessions, bold or heartrending, but always acted, always performed, would all contribute to trying to sketch out an *identikit*, a broad psychological portrait, the mythological, archetypal need that man has always had to play-act, to reinvent himself, to pretend to be another before someone who will stay and listen and believe him.

I can see the master of ceremonies at this extravagant round table performed by a personality like [Roberto] Benigni, and why not himself in person! His air of the eternal student, idealist intellectual, his outrageous insistence on things, his way of espousing or trying to put over rash, bizarre conclusions, and also his extraordinary talent as an actor, in mimicking styles, cadences, characters, personalities, could make him a taunting seminar leader, and the seminar, at his prodding or interruption, and his caricatural and gibing tones, would end up as a colossal parody of all the debates, encounters, face-to-faces, the tribunals that for the past hundred years television has continued to pass on to us daily.

To us, those of our generation, when did actors make their first appearance? Who were the actors when we were children? Where did

34

they come from? Majeroni, Febo Mari, Gustavo Giorgi, Moissi: these were the signatures written with a flourish across large photographs of stern-looking people with flashing eyes, bitter smiles, commanding profiles and long, flowing hair which sometimes fell nearly to the shoulders, like Majeroni's in *Ghosts*. These regal and romantic countenances appeared suddenly on a winter's morning, usually just before Carnival, on the fronts of houses, in the windows of the Caffè Commercio, on the square, at the station, and from up there they looked at us without seeing us, like divinities beyond reach, promising that just maybe they would have come to pay us a visit, they would have materialized. A gift from the gods to our poor, sleepy, forgotten town.

I really believed they were supernatural beings, another race, and the Albergo Leon d'Oro which accommodated them for a few nights acquired the mythical proportions of Olympus. We all looked on with envy at the hotel concierge, who could see them up close, spoke to them, handed them their keys. I could not image what an actor's life could be off the stage or the white movie screen. I had had the fortune to see Majeroni standing erect at the counter of the Dovesi pastry shop, with a long, white silk scarf, a pearl-gray Homburg on his head, a faint trace of makeup, sipping through a straw something steaming hot from a small glass with a silver handle. Mandarin punch, the waiter told us later.

So I had gotten an idea of what Majeroni's life could have been like offstage, but the others, all the others, when the great red curtain closed on the wonders that I had seen and the rude lights came up in the theater to illuminate our same old faces, where did all the actors go? This vague impression of their unreal lives has stuck with me to this day in

my relations with actors, and I do not mind this at all. It seems more helpful to my work. I feel I understand them better, have insight into them at a more intimate level. I have never had any problems with actors, I like their defects, vanity, neurotic side, their psychology—at times childlike, at times a little schizoid.

I am very grateful for what they do for me, and I am always a little bit amazed that the intangible phantasms that I have lived with for months in the realm of the imagination have now come to life, in flesh and blood; they talk, they walk, they smoke, they do what I tell them to, they say their lines, just as I had imagined when little by little I created them.

In these notes I also want to write about the impression that theater made on me the first time I discovered it. When I was 12, I lived in a small house with a yard in front. The large vegetable patch that occupied the back yard bordered on an enormous building—an army barracks? a church?—on which was scrawled in white letters forming a semicircle: "Poli ... ama riminese." Two letters were missing, dropped, lost. Since our family vegetable patch was sunken, the land upon which the building behind the wall enclosure rested seemed higher, way up there.

One morning, I was in the vegetable patch constructing a bow with a reed, when suddenly there was a deafening noise like a railway disaster. It was the enormous shutter of the theater rolling up, which I had never noticed before. Finally, an immense, black opening appeared. In the middle were a man wearing a beret and a raincoat and a woman knitting. A dialogue was being continued. The man: "The murderer must have come in through the window." The woman: "The window is closed." The man: "Sergeant Jonathan found signs that the window had been forced."

Then the man turned to me in the vegetable patch: "Are there figs in that tree?" "I don't know." They were rehearsing a *Grand Guignol*, the company of Bella-Starace-Sainati. Helped up by the man's hands, I entered the dark cavern: I saw the gilt boxes, and coming at me, the belly of a locomotive suspended on ropes, fluttering, among red, white, and yellow celluloids. It was the theater.

Then the man went on with the problem of the window. I did not understand if it was a game or what. A long time must have passed. All of a sudden, my mother's voice called me back. "Soup's on the table." "He's here," said the man with the beret, answering my mother, and he helped me back over the low wall.

Two evenings later, my parents took me to the show. My mother says that I did not budge for the whole performance. The locomotive was advancing from the dark background, from the night; it was about to run over the woman lashed to the tracks, until the woman was saved while an enormous, heavy, soft, red curtain fell over her. The emotion lasted the whole night. During the intermissions, I had seen the wings, the orchestra seats, the velvet, the brass, the aisles, mysterious passageways. I scampered through them all like a mouse.

* * *

The appointed place, then, the fixed setting where the two or three very short films could be shown, is the interior of a theater, with the orchestra covered with an enormous white canvas cloth making it seem a stormy sea, or a field covered with snow, the dark boxes with their glittering gold, the colossal chandelier with its thousands of crystal drops which is sometimes slowly raised up beyond the ceiling to disappear in a mysterious dimension beneath the roof, an enormous, dark and dusty attic loft that is called the

"chandelier pit." It is there, in fact, where the glassy hot-air balloon dwells in the darkness, when no show is on and the entire theater lies silently in the deepest shadows, held up on heavy pulleys awaiting the gala evening when all the boxes are illuminated and it, with an intense plying of ropes and pulleys held all around the void by five or six men, is lowered slowly with a great tinkling of crystals until it emerges from its trap door and stops high on the ceiling in a blaze of gems and beams like a shining sun as deserving of applause as the most dazzling star of the company.

Our actors, too, applaud, their gaze directed upward. Then, while from above the voices of the workers resound, little by little the confused, low talking of the onlookers, whose words we cannot make out, dies down, vanishes. Someone smokes, another reads the newspaper, and in this expectant atmosphere, flat and indifferent, the telecamera suddenly zooms in on one of the figures: the face, swollen and reddened from broken blood vessels, of Marcello, who after a long silence during which he simply looks into the lens with moist, red-rimmed eyes, asks with a slightly awkward smile if he can have a drop of something. They hand him a small glass; he drinks and with a satisfied smile clears his throat and starts to talk, hoarse and shortwinded.

"A drop can pick you up. Especially on these occasions ..." (He stops, looking around with an air intended to be conspiratorial, amused, but which instead colors his face with a desperate and roguish expression. He gulps and in a lower tone, as if talking to himself, goes on.) "I should never have accepted, and what did I not know? I knew, just as I knew my part, but my memory is failing. I used to know all the parts I have played, the prompter, the hunchbacks at the movie theaters, never wanted them!" (He fumbles for something in his pockets, his handkerchief. He dries his slightly teary eyes, blows his nose and continues.) "Telephone numbers? I never had an address book, then one day I found myself with the phone receiver up to my ear. I heard the phone ringing but couldn't remember whom I had called. 'Who's speaking?' I asked politely. 'And who are you—you're the one who called!' I didn't feel like saying who and I hung up. I'm an actor and to have my memory on the blink is not such a great thing."

He goes on with this unashamed, pathetic, amusing and heartrending monologue of a man who spies on old age and in turn is spied upon, followed closely, shadowed, observed by it. He tells, for example, of how, when he leaves his bedroom, on tiptoe, he closes the door and waits for a minute, then throws open the door again and sticks his head in, sniffing deeply to see if the room where he sleeps smells of old age. And shadows? But doesn't it seem to you that our shadows age before we do? Often at night, walking in the middle of the street, with the lamps that alternate patches of light with others of semi-darkness, my shadow seemed shorter, more crooked, more hunched. Sometimes I'd ask myself, staring at it in the absolute silence of the night: how old would you say that shadow is?

And the mirror ... by treachery, especially the ones on the street, when with a horrified start you realize that that passerby is yourself. The first time a girl gave him her seat on the bus; the headline on the local news page: "Old Man Run Over in Crossing Zone," then upon reading it you discover that the man is forty-six years old. And his circumspect, cautious questions to find out how old the taxi driver is without directly touching on the subject, and judging from his face, he decides he is definitely very old, decrepit; in the end,

he finds out that the man is ten years younger than himself.

To create the greatest effect with this embarrassing and grotesque confession on the passing seasons, on the trap of old age that it isn't true that it arrives little by little, but suddenly, from one day to the next and then—How's this! Until yesterday, I was always the youngest, at every gathering, group, dinner party and then what happened? When did I let myself be distracted to the point of not realizing that now I'm always the oldest? To make this candid and desperate outpouring all the more poignant, I think it would be effective to realize at a certain point that the actor who is confessing all this with such sincerity is seated in the corner of a railway car; and since it is nighttime outside, the window reflects his face.

Here, I have jotted down as they come to me situations that could enhance the episode.

Some figures who have been silently dozing in a corner, get up with their bundles and get off when the incomprehensible name of a station is bellowed out in the dark.

"How old can they have been?" our actor wonders. And the journey resumes. Outside the window, in the darkness of the countryside or beneath the illuminated platform roofing of small stations immediately swallowed up by the dark, some figures appeared for an instant, men and women whom our hero thinks for a minute to have recognized, recalled. He waves his arms to greet them; he wants to lean out the window and ask why. "Once, during a spiritual séance, the medium said that there was a being who wished to speak with me. It had to be my father. Very ill-at-ease, I asked him what human language was like in the dimension he was in now that he had passed away. And he answered that the impression was the same as when he was alive and during his work, at night, he thought of his wife, children, all of us, and the train kept running in the night taking him further and further away."

The ticket collector could be a doctor who takes his blood pressure and listens to his heart. Then, when he is alone again and outside the windows there are no longer any fields or cities, but just the milky whiteness of the dawn, a beautiful, stupendous women enters. "Finally!" murmurs the traveler, with a smile dangling on his lips.

It is to be hoped that the episode sketched out above may be appropriately developed. For now it is just a cue that may be taken to construct a sequence for Mastroianni.

At the end, the colleagues applaud; they congratulate him, and Benigni makes a few criticisms. The other colleagues make more or less favorable comments, but each one has something of his own to say about old age, Marcello's interpretation of it, about the script, and everyone wonders who the beautiful lady is who entered the compartment at the end. Some say that they would have done it better and, in general, all complain about the roles assigned. Among others, Giulietta Masina claims that she has always wanted to do roles completely different from those she has had to do. Romantic roles, she says, the kind where you wear beautiful clothes; touching love stories with scenes and musical themes that move you to tears. There, an episode could be invented for Giulietta that tells in a comic vein about the tense, quarrelsome, at times even violent, relationship between director and actors. Widely divergent approaches to a part, ways of perceiving a character, and then the disputes, rifts, insults, threats of abandonment, the anger, the humiliation, the actress's demands that the director act out for her the female role, mocking him in front of everybody ....

1. The Curtain

It protects, hides, covers, marks the end but also the beginning. What is it, who is on the other side of the curtain? What awaits us, who? The curtain seen as an almost natural operation to interrupt, suspend, cancel. How many real-life situations could be solved with the providential "curtain falling"? Difficult, annoying relationships, embarrassing, unbearable situations, illnesses, tensions, responsibilities that crush you, put a hunch in your back ... everything magically disappears with the curtain falling.

Or, on the contrary, the raising of the great curtain reveals to you panoramas, situations, worlds, people, wonderful places, extremely pleasant, exciting, unexpected ... new stories, new places, thrilling feminine beauty, divinities, terrestrial paradises.

2. To live constantly pursued, observed, spied on, watched, chased by a troupe

A group of people with lights, microphones, mirrors, cosmetic tissues, powder, grease paint, hair combs. And always that resounding, metallic voice, amplified by loud speakers that suggests, orders, corrects, threatens, coaxes, chides, commands to repeat, redo, run through again, try again, say again, until the imperious shout to stop, which immobilizes, switches off, collapses everything.
Words of love to the camera. In bed with the camera.

3. The public

From the dressing room, the actor's refuge and defense, a murmur can already be heard in the distance, an indistinct buzz whose echo reveals a carefreeness, a nonchalance, the pleasure of being together, meeting friends, to consume the entertainment (how he, too, would like to be among those free, blissful people, unconcerned, unafraid of examinations, indeed to the contrary, who are there to judge!).

And this easy, low talk is now a little noisier, and the actor on the empty stage, hidden by the curtain, seeks in that ocean of faces out there the face of some friend. Unfamiliar faces, undecipherable attitudes and expressions. Even the faces of the people sitting in the first rows seem not to communicate anything comforting, well disposed, tolerant. The audience as a whole, beneath the light of the great chandelier, suggests the idea that it is made up of creatures of another race, from another planet, who have all come down together from a spaceship to invade those seats, those boxes, those galleries.

The lights go off all at once, the audience disappears. Now it is just a shapeless mass, breathing out there in the darkness; you sense only the thousands of eyes directed toward the empty stage on which you, the actor, must presently appear .... How comforting the view is of the silhouettes of the stagehands and the electricians in the shadows of the forward wings from the other part of that free zone, exposed, illuminated, that is the stage. If only you could join them, running across the stage and hiding among them, asking protection.

(Sensation of finding oneself at sea at night, alone, on a raft that is drifting toward the unknown. What silence, what solitude! Exactly that of the shipwrecked person or the astronaut. What a relief to see that little flame lit in the darkness of a box. Who could it be? A friend? Someone who will applaud?)

Hoots, whistles, hurling of coins, carrots, an enormous rat, which has lived with me ever since that time they threw it at me on the stage. There he is, over there.

4. The shelter of the dressing room

The mirror, the grease paint, the dressing gown, and all those faces, at times of strangers, who between one act and the other lean in to shake your hand, hug you, ask you questions that you can't make out in all that confusion.

40

Below, I have listed the settings and constructions necessary to develop the story of the television special:

a) The empty studio. In the background, tripods with lights, a clothes stand on wheels with various stage costumes hung up on it (these are the costumes that the protagonist will wear in the various sequences). Pushed up almost against the wall, a makeup table with all the necessary accessories, including an arc of lights strung in the frame.

Enter the protagonist, who sits down on the makeup chair, and, prompted by some questions, speaks of actors, telling of when he saw an actor's face for the first time.

In the same studio, in a corner filled with thick fog, the appearance of posters, placards, theater bills portraying the aristocratic, demoniacal, and languid faces of actors and actresses.

b) The interior of a theater in miniature, a "model as if seen from the stage": orchestra, boxes, chandelier. A classical, late-nineteenth-century theater such as the Valle or the Argentina may be taken as an example.

c) A vast and deep platform that will represent the stage of a theater with backdrops, wings, the prompter's box, orchestra well and the first three rows of seats. The sumptuous red velvet curtain with gold fringe.

Note: This construction is particularly important as it is here that most of the special's scenes will develop.

1. The railroad with the approach of the train that is about to run over the woman lashed to the tracks.

2. On the large, completely empty stage, now Paolo speaks of the public: this mysterious, invisible entity crouching in the dark which can be heard breathing, coughing. For the actor on the stage, it is like finding oneself before a bottomless chasm, or at sea in the night, seen from the bow of a ship, or the cosmos for an astronaut lost in space.

How comforting is the prompter's box! In his desperate solitude, the actor envies the peace, the security, the comfort of whoever can live in that warm little well, with his back to the public, ignoring it ... oh, to be in his place!

Now, the protagonist is before the mirror, with the makeup artist and hairdresser behind him. He talks about old age.

3. The train compartment, with the little scene between the protagonist and the stranger.

Exterior in the countryside at night
(this may be the only exterior in the film)
A stretch of railroad, where we see the tail lights of a train drawing away in the distance.

Note: in the same exterior, that same night, we may also shoot the appearance of the Rolls Royce.

Another solution for this scene could be to shoot it in a theater: a black backdrop would be enough to suggest the expanse of fields in the night. To decide.

Similarly, it is to decide if it would be better to shoot the interior of the Rolls using a real car or to construct a model and furnish it appropriately.

d) Miniature model of a castle illuminated by the headlights of the Rolls.

For the dinner at the castle scene, I am undecided as to whether it would be better to build the setting on our stage or to shoot the scene in an interior location to be found in a real castle or palazzo.

c) 4. On the usual stage: a large chandelier suspended over the dining room table in the castle, to which the protagonist clings to escape his host's ferocious mastiffs. A little talk about the comic actor, and paradoxical situations.

5. The stunts teacher (falling, tumbling, and other dangerous situations) shows the protagonist how to slip, fall, and roll to the ground without hurting himself.

a. 2. Empty theater: Again the protagonist is seated on the makeup chair, where efforts are being made to make him resemble Jiggs. Next to him are 2 or 3 candidates for the role of Maggie.

c) The sets for the Jiggs story will be mounted on the stage. They are in order:

- Parlor for the concert at home with Maggie
- Exterior facade of apartment with Jiggs
- Sidewalk of the same building, where Jiggs lands inside the bricklayer's bucket
- Interior of a bar with Jiggs's friends

Note: the sequence of the transvestite is still undecided. In any case, I have made a few notes (in case it is necessary) on the constructions to build, again in the theater.

On the outskirts of a city, a stretch of asphalted street flanked by embankments and rugged, scrubby fields; bound in the background by large public housing buildings etched against the stormy night sky by thousands of lit windows.

In a car stopped beneath a lamp are the protagonist and a transvestite. It's raining. Other grotesque, squalid characters mill around, heating their bare or fishnet-stockinged legs at small wood fires.

[The short scene is suggested by the protagonist who, when asked the question, "Which character role would you like to play?" answered "Professor Unrat from the *Blue Angel*," with the only difference being that instead of the night-club vamp played by Marlene Dietrich, in my version there is a transvestite.]

(I was forgetting the short sequence of the ring.)

Practically, from the makeup chair, the protagonist, having heard again the sound of the typical boxing match gong, sets out accompanied by the usual people on such occasions (seconds, trainers, journalists) in a confused and boisterous shouting toward ... the ring, which, violently lit by large shaded lamps that hang from the ceiling, has the air of an executioner's scaffold.

Paolo, dazed, out of breath, with a bruised and swollen eye (which we saw the makeup artist create), walks through a long, narrow aisle between the tiers of a ferociously screaming crowd .... The entire scene has the sinister air of an execution.

(Note: I must remember that during other scenes of the special, we have heard the gong ring every once and a while, and each time the protagonist has given a start, white in the face and hurrying to change the subject.)

The stage (the platform) is the scene on which much of the special unfolds. The protagonist, sweaty and staggering, hops and runs around the ring, bouncing off the cords; his adversary, enormous, gigantic, implacable, follows him and pounds him.

But there could be even more than one adversary, and not all of them boxers: there are also a few film producers, someone from the public who bluntly tells him that he's had enough of Villaggio; and why not a woman, a former love? and a couple of lawyers, a tax agent .... Between one swing and the next, Paolo, bathed in sweat, dazed, groggy, also has to answer the questions of a journalist who is by his side and follows him, or better, chases him all over the ring.

JOURNALIST: What is comedy for you? What excites you the most? When did you decide to become an actor? What do you think of television?

The ring is full of people. And they are all chasing Paolo; they move as if on a dance floor, colliding, elbowing, pushing one another. The public screams, begins to clamor, whistle, throw banana skins, coconut husks.

Panting, gasping, holding the shreds of a tuxedo and a battered top hat in their hands, the Makeup Man, the Costumer and the Hairdresser violently push their way through

42 the crowd. They enter the ring and get to Paolo, who is suffocated in the middle of a real crowd, and drag him to the corner, forcing him to sit down. Someone yells that he must get ready for the final scene; he must put on the clown shoes, they have to make him up and put the red putty on his nose, conceal his bruises and replace them with the vertical line typical of the clown face.

An assistant arrives with an old trombone and hands it to Paolo, who sets out followed by a small procession, blowing kisses left and right and bidding farewell in a loud voice:

PAOLO: Good-bye! I'm leaving! I'll be in touch! Addio! Addio!

As far as the final scene is concerned, I still do not have very clear ideas. I think, however, that I can anticipate that it could develop in a circus ring, where the protagonist, made up as a clown, plays on a tuba a classic circus melody, clownish and heartrending. At the center of the ring is a spaceship. The protagonist takes his leave of everyone, shaking the hands of the workers, stagehands, electricians, assistants, and then he enters the cockpit of the science-fiction construction, which takes off with a whistling noise toward interstellar space.

Now we see our hero curled up in a fetal position in the cramped cockpit of the spaceship; he looks out of the windows at the starry firmament. A device rings insistently like a telephone. It *is* a telephone. They are calling from earth to ask him when he's coming back.

PAOLO: Are Craxi, Occhetto, Moussa, and Peter still down there?

[And after listening to the answer in silence, he shakes his head with emphasis.]

PAOLO: Then I'm staying here!

And he breaks off any communication with the wretched planet.

Let's see which of the old ideas can be saved, bearing in mind that now there is a single actor: Villaggio.

I would begin like this: the empty theater; at the back we can make out some people standing still as if they are waiting; others, electricians maybe, are putting some spotlights on scaffolding or tripods placed here and there.

As we get closer, on mobile clothes stands we can distinguish costumes, clothes, robes, shirts, and, on shelves, hats in various styles. In a corner, there is a makeup table, surmounted by a mirror, in the frame of which several bulbs that are out. A male figure (Paolo Villaggio) crosses the dark area of the theater, making for the part that is illuminated by the spotlights.

"There he is!" someone says, turning to look at the celebrity who has now reached the circle of people and is waving to them.

A girl, seated next to a small table on which some sheets of paper are scattered, begins to prompt, reading from a script:

ASSISTANT: Hello, excuse me, but outside I have just met....

Paolo, who has entered the most brightly illuminated area, turns his head first one way, then the other in greeting, but with a forced smile on his face. He repeats mechanically:

PAOLO: Hello, excuse me, but outside I have just met....

Then he dries up and with some embarrassment looks at the prompter. The girl says a few more sentences, which Paolo does not seem to understand. Perhaps he has not heard them.

PAOLO: What? I don't understand. For the last few mornings, when I get up I've had a buzzing noise....

ASSISTANT: A buzzing noise in my ear....

Then, turning towards someone who is sitting next to her:

He knows it, he knows it, he remembers it....

He smiles nervously and shakes his head in irritation.

PAOLO: No, on the contrary, I don't remember anything!

The buzz....

He looks around, genuinely bewildered.

PAOLO: Shall I go on?

He begins to speak more quietly, as if he were soliloquizing.

PAOLO: What harm is there in admitting it? My memory has gone, together with a lot of other things. I used to remember everything. I've never carried a diary. Phones, for example....

Continuing like this, he approaches the girl holding the script and cranes his neck in order to read it. Then he grabs it from her, flicks through the pages, and gives it back to her; he sits down, resigned and disheartened, as if he wants to give up. He remains silent for some time, hanging his head. Then he slowly raises his face and stares at us, so that we can see real discomfort in his eyes, and this uneasiness is combined with a feeling of shame. All around, there is total silence. Someone, the makeup man, approaches Paolo and politely speaks to him:

MAKEUP MAN: Would you like to come over here?

Paolo starts, nods, then gets up and follows him over to the makeup table, where an assistant and a hairdresser turn the chair toward the actor.

HAIRDRESSER: Coffee, Signor Villaggio? With two croissants?

Paolo shakes his head, slumping into the chair.

PAOLO: No croissants, thank you, no coffee either. A glass of lemon juice....

Then with an ironical smile, almost a sneer

Yes, it's a new diet.

The sheet of paper in his hand falls to the floor. He bends down to pick it up, but the assistant makeup man beats him to it. Paolo thanks him, and, as if he were continuing his previous soliloquy, says:

PAOLO: There you are, this is another sign, beside my failing memory. If I drop something, before picking it up, I have to think about it!

To the makeup man:

Tell me the truth, do I smell of old age? I always put myself to the test, in the morning, when I come out of my room: I close the door, then I suddenly open it again, and I sniff to see if the room, the bed where I have slept, smells of old age.

He raises an arm as if he wants to smell his armpits, but he stops halfway because the makeup man has placed a babyish wig on his head, with bangs that almost cover his eyebrows.

MAKEUP MAN: I've also got a blond one, Signor Paolo; were you fair or dark when you were a kid?

PAOLO: Actually I was brown. But let me try on the blond one.

He himself takes it from the head of the mannequin on which it has been placed, putting it on his own head with comical results.

PAOLO: You know I've got a photo taken when I was nine...

He points to himself in the mirror.

I was just like this!

MAKEUP MAN: A handsome kid!

ASSISTANT: *She discreetly begins to prompt again:*

Well then, the actor; when did I notice or realize that men and women called actors existed?

Paolo nods at each word, repeating it in his head in order to remember it. Then, he looks around, as if he were seeking the person who has asked him the question:

PAOLO: I can remember the first time as if it were only yesterday. It was winter. The small town where I was born is swallowed up by the fog in winter. I was with Lasagna, my schoolmate; we were walking along the avenue that led to the sea. We couldn't see a thing; from afar we could hear the hoarse foghorns of the boats that were trying to enter the port. We walked straight into something metallic: it was a billboard, and when we stepped back with our hands on our foreheads, we saw,

through the thick fog, the large face of an old man with long curly hair protruding from an artist's beret; his eyes were madeup, and a bitter, yet inviting, smile played on his lips. His name was written across his face: Achille Majeroni.

This was how actors were heralded in my town before they arrived at the Politeama, which was the only large theater.

A number of posters depicting characters with severe expressions, flashing eyes, and imperious profiles appear in double exposure.

PAOLO'S VOICE: Regal, romantic faces that, in winter, shortly before carnival, appear on the facades of the houses, in the windows of the Caffè Commercio, in the square, at the station, looking down on us like remote divinities, without seeing us. It was a promise that they would come to see us, they would materialize. A gift from the gods to our poor, sleepy, forgotten town....

These are sequences that could follow:

a) Paolo remembers when, as a child (also with the blond wig), his parents took him to the theater: the magic, the enchantment of the seats covered with red velvet; the chandelier, suspended from the ceiling high above, with its glittering glass drops; the boxes where, in the darkness, elegant men and beautiful women could be glimpsed.

Paolo's voice will accompany these images, giving a moving description of those distant times.

A typical *Grand Guignol* is being presented: on the stage, a woman, whose hands and feet are bound, is laid on a railroad track. It is the dead of night; in the distance, the noise of a train is heard as it approaches inexorably.... To tumultuous applause the curtain drops, hiding the fantastic world, the terrible scene; but, almost at once, it slowly opens again to reveal, in a blaze of light, the actors, who thank us, bowing and blowing kisses. And they are all there: the heroine who has been saved at the very last moment by her handsome fiancé, the engineer who has managed to stop the tremendous, smoke-belching locomotive just a yard from the woman abandoned on the track, the stationmaster and two or three other characters, all glowing with radiant smiles. And when Paolo says, "I, too, would like to have been up there, enjoying the loud, enthusiastic, genuinely grateful applause...," we see him (still with bangs, wearing a sailor suit, with a confirmation ribbon on his arm) as, deeply moved and intensely happy, he bows to the audience and gazes enraptured at the beautiful actress next to him, who is blowing kisses to everyone.

These living puppets aroused a certain amount of fear; heavily madeup, their strained smiles and their flashing eyes conveyed a sense of uneasiness, of alienation. Who are they? Who dwells in them?

The audience

THE JOURNALIST COMMENTS

JOURNALIST: Oh yes, the audience, when it has a good time, is extremely gratified. It's a real friend, warm-hearted, affectionate, grateful, it loves you, it makes you feel fit and strong, it makes life more bearable.

PAOLO: Yes, that's true, applause nurtures, cures, it's better than any medicine. How often I've gone on stage with a temperature; the first round of applause was enough to get rid of it. When I'm at home, too, when I wake up with a bout of flu, I ask the neighbor's family, or the janitor's, to come to the door of my room; they applaud and I feel fine! But ... when the audience is silent ... a silence that is like that of a starless night ... you feel as if the sea is before you, you know it's there, you can feel it breathing, moving....

For Benigni (Pinocchio)

But *who* is the audience, this headless monster squatting in the obscurity, this throbbing darkness, this mirror in which the actor scrutinizes himself, this entity to which he is sacrificed? Let's listen to what Benigni has to say; perhaps we have already met him hanging from the chandelier, up there in the dusty vault, among the thousand glass drops that shine like a glittering spaceship above the audience of which he is so fond.

I would like Roberto to play the part of Pinocchio. While they are making him up as a puppet behind the scenes, amidst crates, trunks, ropes, and winches, Benigni talks about his relationship with the audience (*pubblico* in Italian), which is almost a physical, sensual one, to the extent that he calls it *pubblica* (giving the masculine noun a nonexistent feminine form). He would like to throw himself into it, embrace everybody, one at a time, be on first-name terms with them, and go back with them to their homes.

And while they're making up Roberto, nearby and at the same time, the actress who will play the Blue Fairy is being selected. She needs to be a young girl, aged between fifteen and seventeen, with blue-tinted hair and the self-possessed expression of a girlish mother, sweet and tender, but also severe. Who will be chosen?

When Pinocchio is ready, he meets Lampwick (Lucignolo) at the edge of the village while he waits for the coach drawn by donkeys and driven by the nasty Coachman (Omino di Burro), who could also very well be played by Paolo Villaggio.

The sad fate of the disobedient puppet will be to spend the rest of his life as a donkey in a circus. The ringmaster, once again Paolo Villaggio, wearing boots and a frock coat, with whip in hand, soon makes all these asses—Pinocchio has been turned into one of them—toe the line.

In a box by the ring, the Blue Fairy watches him sorrowfully.

Who have I chosen to play this part? Why yes, Francesca Dellera. Who could be a better

Blue Fairy for Pinocchio-Benigni? The actress in question is truly fascinating: her beauty is so showy that it is almost comic; she is a big doll-like creature on whom the pallor of her skin and her made-up eyes confer a vaguely funereal seductiveness.

Struck by these eyes rather than the severe ringmaster's whip, Pinocchio the donkey falls to his knees, in the ring, braying and crying desperately in front of the Fairy, this female figure that is mother, betrothed, spouse, schoolmistress, Madonna, and also Italy—why not, a turreted Italy, with a tricolor veil, the downtrodden, neglected, barbarized motherland.

"How beautiful you are, Italy!" Benigni could exclaim, "If only you were really like this! 'Oh Patria mia, vedo le mura e gli archi / e le colonne e i simulacri e l'erme / torri degli avi nostri, / ma la gloria non vedo....' (O my country, I see the walls and the arches / And the columns and the simulacra and the solitary / Towers of our forefathers, / But I do not see the glory....)," he recites, mournfully intoning Leopardi's refined invective (or other lines, other indignant statements by Giusti, Carducci, or Aleardi).

And he could continue with one of his outbursts of political satire, a bitter tirade against the present sad state of our nation, the general decay, the pollution of our seas, the arrogance of those in power, the corruption, the cultural decline.
Thus, the poor Pinocchio-donkey sobs and brays.

And maybe the invective redeems him, because the Fairy, appreciating his sincere repentance, turns the donkey back into a humanized puppet.

Then the ring comes to life again, and the actors, accompanied by the joyful cracks of Villaggio's whip, pour into it in a great procession. It is a final parade to the staccato rhythm of a circus march, and all together—including Jiggs and Maggie, the Blue Fairy, the Brazilian transvestite, Gassman, Giulietta, Marcello, Lampwick, and Coachman, they smile and thank the audience in the blaze of the ring spotlights and the great glass chandelier, which, high above, gradually goes out and returns languidly into its cavern, immobile and opaque as a celestial monster.

Characters in the special

Makeup man—Assistant
Hairdresser—Assistant
Workmen—Stagehands—Electricians

Actors in the *Grand Guignol* Company
Girl tied to the track
Engineer
Stoker
Savior
Another 2 or 3 characters in the *Grand Guignol* company

Stranger who travels in the train with Paolo
Chauffeur of the Rolls Royce
Beautiful lady in the Rolls
Butler and servants in the castle
Husband of the beautiful lady
Stunt instructor
Beautiful girls who appear at night on Paolo's bedside table

Maggie and her aristocratic friends
Pianist
Jiggs's friends
Transvestite
Other transvestites
Policemen
A couple of passers-by
Referee of the boxing match
Opposing boxer (or boxers)
Seconds
Coaches
Journalist

Characters:
Paolo Villaggio in various parts
Assistant (perhaps more than one)
Makeup man
Assistant makeup man
Actor of the *Grand Guignol*
Elderly stranger in the train compartment
Maggie
Maggie's snobbish friends
Jiggs's friends
Journalist
Beautiful women on the magic bedside table

notte
piova

scompartimento
tenoviario

Notes for the scene of the encounter on the train

The scene could start with some of the thoughts that come to Paolo's mind when, because of his work, or when he's shaving, or just by chance, he looks at himself in a mirror and, as always, notes that he does not like his face.

What kind of face would he like to have? That of John Barrymore? In the mirror, the countenance of the famous American actor is superimposed on that of Paolo.

Or else that of Edgar Allan Poe? There is the same superimposition, and lo and behold, the handsome visage, romantic and funereal, of the *poète maudit*.

Other virile countenances follow, fascinating and mysterious; when they vanish, and Paolo's face reappears, they only make the contrast even more evident and increase his disappointment.

Paolo carefully examines himself: he lifts an eyebrow with a finger, he covers his double chin and part of his cheeks with a hand, he ruffles his hair, he looks at himself in profile, then in a three-quarter position; finally, he dims the light, doing his best to appear different to himself, and more acceptable. It is during this anxious, desperate self-scrutiny that Paolo discovers dullness, fatigue, discoloration, weaknesses, wrinkles, and other signs of wear and tear in his eyes and skin that he had not previously noticed.

PAOLO: How wrong the makeup artists are, when, in order to make up an actor as an old man, they insist on drawing wrinkles and giving him a bald pate! And aren't we actors slaves to the same convention in our belief that, to convey the idea of old age, it is enough to speak with a hoarse voice, make our hands tremble, and walk with an unsteady gait?

No, the process of aging means becoming another person, someone we don't know, that we've never set eyes on.

While Paolo is speaking, we realize that we are now in a second-class train compartment. It is night, and Paolo is sitting in a corner near the window streaked with rain. The speed of the train makes the drops run horizontally; in them, every now and again, the scattered lights of the countryside are broken up into myriad rays.

Paolo continues to speak:

PAOLO: It's another person! That's the old man! That's you as an old man! Quite another person, who's arrived unexpectedly, without being announced; he suddenly comes into your life, and he's you, he's me!

Paolo is staring, incredulous and frightened, at a traveler seated directly opposite him; like him, he is being rocked to and fro by the swaying of the train. The stranger holds his head slightly back, letting it rest on the seat, and although, from time to time, the compartment light moves away from his face, leaving it in shadow, we see that he is an elderly man, and that he does not look at all like Paolo. In fact, he does not even remotely resemble him. With his long, thin fingers he is stroking an eyebrow, and he gazes absent-mindedly at the patterns of the raindrops on the window. Paolo continues to stare at him, holding his breath and seeking in amazement, in anguish, a feature, a gesture, an expression, something in which he can recognize himself. No, there's nothing that resembles him. He is really another person, and Paolo blurts out a phrase, an attempt at rebellion in which the keynote is indignation and dejection.

PAOLO: No, it's not me.

The stranger looks at Paolo with a hint of a smile, in which it is possible to detect a feeling of comprehension, a note of gentle irony. But his eyes have a look of extraneousness, of inhuman indifference.

PAOLO: But how did this happen? You didn't warn me, you didn't let me know. Yes, there have been some signs, some portents, but this is going too far...

What does the doctor say now? I mean, at your, at our age?

The other man takes a small tin of tablets out of his pocket. He puts one in his mouth and offers one to Paolo, who seems about to accept mechanically, but then makes a gesture of refusal with his hand, as if to say that if the result is the individual sitting in front of him, what is the point of continuing to take them?

PAOLO: Still? Do I still have to take them?

And looking at the other man's hands, which are wrinkled and covered with brown marks, asks him:

PAOLO: Can I see how long your skin takes, when it's been squeezed and raised, to become flat again?

The stranger complies with his request, pinching the back of his hand and pulling up the skin, which remains raised for a considerable length of time, while Paolo, disheartened and repentant, murmurs:

PAOLO: Still? Is it still up? Won't it go down? Excuse me.

They look at each other in silence for some time. Then Paolo asks:

PAOLO: But, um, do you remember me?

The other man is silent. He still has an indecipherable smile, and he gently nods his head in sympathy. No doubt he considers the question to be quite unnecessary. But Paolo refuses to give up. He is deeply distressed and bewildered, and he opens his mouth a couple of times, as if he urgently wants to say something. He is stopped by a violent coughing fit of the other man, who immediately seeks to reassure Paolo with a gesture of his hands. Lowering his head, Paolo rests his hands on his legs and murmurs:

PAOLO: Isn't there anything I can do to slow down, to stop, this decay?

The other man strokes the back of his hand, where the skin has finally returned to its original form:

STRANGER: *With a mild, resigned air* Oh, no. In any case, if we had known about it, and we'd taken some precautions, we would never have met.

PAOLO: What a lot of questions I would like to ask you! But I'm afraid. There are so many people I would like to ask you about—but no, I prefer not to know.

The stranger, after a moment of silence that seems to approve of this decision, asks with a hint of amused curiosity:

STRANGER: Not even about ... about...?

Paolo appears to have understood to whom he is referring, and he listens anxiously, leaning forward, hopeful and fearful at the same time; meanwhile, the stranger, whose shoulders have begun to shake in a fit of silent laughter, makes gestures with his hands, indicating that what has happened is truly inconceivable. He holds his head between his hands and leans forward, continuing to laugh silently, overwhelmed by uncontrollable mirth.

Paolo, too, begins to laugh, and, feeling more optimistic, he says approvingly:

PAOLO: Oh, good, I can see that it's put you in a good mood!

The other man nods, still shaken by laughter, and now he waves both his arms like a person who is attempting to describe something that is inconceivable, but immediately gives up, and, even if he could do so, the reality of the situation goes beyond, way beyond, the power of his imagination....

The stranger leans toward Paolo, as if he were about to fall, and continues to shake his head, but more slowly than before. His fit of laughter has ended. The man remains immobile, leaning forward, then he raises the palms of his hands to his eyes and rubs them at length.

Paolo is still chuckling, while the stranger slowly straightens up and sits back in his corner, where, overcome by despondency, he begins to weep.

Paolo looks around as if he feels trapped. Fi-

nally he springs to his feet, opens the compartment door, and goes out into the corridor. The train slows down, then it stops. In the deserted corridor, he is about to make his way toward the door of the car. He does not want to look toward the compartment again; he freezes for a moment, then moves with decision, muttering to himself:

PAOLO: Isn't it about time I stopped having these gloomy fantasies?

Turning his head just slightly before he opens the door, he murmurs:

PAOLO: Goodbye.

The actor could ask his mysterious traveling companion (himself in ten year's time, so aged that he has become unrecognizable, and even seems to be another person) for his phone number. The two men exchange numbers, and the actor looks at his double as, with trembling hand, he writes his number on a card; and seeing him so bald, bent, and fragile, he is overcome by a feeling of anguish that he seeks to quell, rebelling against the idea and saying to himself: "Isn't it about time I stopped having these gloomy fantasies?"

He gets up with decision, mumbles farewell to the elderly man, and gets off the train in the open countryside. (Etcetera, etcetera, the apparition of an automobile with a beautiful lady.)

Note

The exchange of phone numbers between the two men could perhaps have consequences later on in the story. In a pocket in his jacket, the actor finds the card with the number and tries to call it. Someone replies, and the voice appears to be that of the disconcerting traveling companion, who, however, does not remember him and seems to be annoyed, or else he is so senile that he mumbles incoherent, incomprehensible congratulations, greetings, best wishes to the wife, the children....

"But I....," mutters our protagonist, who is deeply disturbed. He hangs up and, just like the elderly man on the other end of the line, looks at us in dismay.

Here we are, he has got off in the dark countryside. It continues to rain... The train goes off into the distance, and its rhythmic noise gradually becomes weaker. Its rear lights disappear into the darkness.

Where is he? Far off, the barking of a dog can be heard. Then, in the dark, the lights of a large automobile standing in the middle of the countryside go on and off, as if they were winking.

It is a Rolls Royce. A young chauffeur in a splendid new uniform bows politely:

CHAUFFEUR: Maestro, please.

He opens the door, allowing us to glimpse the inside of the luxurious automobile, which is lit up like a drawing room. There is someone sitting on the rear seat, in the corner: a very beautiful and extremely elegant lady. With a regal gesture she invites Paolo to get in.

Paolo bends to kiss the hand that the lady offers him and gets into the fabulous vehicle. The chauffeur has also got in. He turns his head very slightly in order to hear the lady's voice. Softly she murmurs:

LADY: To the castle!

Other themes for Villaggio

One, which recurs throughout the conversation, will be the theme of old age:

"But when did it begin? I was always the youngest, at any dinner party, in any group of people, or at any meeting: why is it that I'm always the oldest now? When was I not paying attention, and it suddenly got hold of me and possessed me, so I'll never get rid of it now? It's not true that you age little by little. No. The wrinkles, the fact that you get unsteadier on your feet day by day, the illnesses, the aches and pains, the hair that falls out or goes white, the muscles that go flabby, the yellowish marks on the skin.... Yes, I realize, they are signs, portents, warnings... but old age arrives suddenly, it grabs you, it gets into your system, it transforms you, and you makeup artists delude yourselves if you think that making up someone as an old man just means drawing wrinkles on his face and giving him a bald pate, and we actors are slaves to the same convention, in our belief that, to convey the idea of old age, it is sufficient to speak with a hoarse voice, make our hands tremble, or have bleary eyes.... This is banal, superficial, a mere caricature, and it's done in bad faith. Once again it's repression, flight... the process of aging means becoming another person... someone you've never seen, someone you've never met, or even imagined. And he doesn't even remotely resemble you. He's another person. That's the old man! That's you as an old man! Quite another person! He's arrived unexpectedly...." (The scene of the train follows.)

First suggestion
In the Rolls Royce, which seems to be waiting for him in the dark countryside, there is a very beautiful woman. A robotlike chauffeur sits at the wheel, stiff and immobile. The actor gets into the car, gazes enraptured at the beautiful lady, and immediately says to her in

transports of admiration and desire: "I know who you are: you are the mysterious lady who, when we arrive with the company in small provincial towns, we actors glimpse in the gloom of the stalls and in the more secretive obscurity of a box. We always hope that after the performance you will pay us a visit in the dressing-room together with the mayor, the prefect, and the most important personages of the town. How often have I wanted to meet you and invite you to dinner at the hotel restaurant. Ah, at last I've met you!"

The lady could reply thus: "But *I* am inviting you to dinner! I live further on, at the castle. I am alone; my husband has gone hunting. He always goes hunting—he leaves me alone for days at a time!"

AT THE CASTLE
The dinner. The woman is a real man-eater. In fact, our protagonist is served at table on a huge tray by silent, impassive waiters. The lady, who has become enormous, looks at him greedily. She licks her lips, parts them, opens her mouth....

ALTERNATIVELY: HER HUSBAND ARRIVES
WITH HIS DOGS
Our protagonist climbs on the table and clings to the great chandelier. In this uncomfortable position, he says: "*This* is the fate of comic actors! Now what must I do, fall into the tureen full of hot soup? My stand-in is wonderful... come on, Danilo, come and replace me."

THE INTERVIEWER'S QUESTION
"But when, on the other hand, you have no choice, because it isn't possible to use a stand-in, how do you manage?"

Stand-in
death on the stage
The actor explains the tricks of the trade: how to fall, how to receive blows, how to pre-

54

tend to take a punch, the contortions to make when you are "shot," before you collapse and "die"...

Oh yes, death on stage in the theater: what a splendid opportunity for the actor's innate histrionic ability!

Just think of *La morte civile*, starring Ermete Zacconi. The gasping, the convulsions, the trembling dashes from one wing to another, the never-ending death throes, the spasms, the jerks of a crazed puppet, the feet kicking at the air, the dribbling, the painful sobs... and then the final collapse on the boards of the stage. But it isn't over yet: the elderly actor rolls like a skittle and risks falling into the orchestra pit. Finally, after another series of tremors, his hands desperately clawing at the air like talons, he becomes still, and at last lies dead. The audience is deeply moved: in ecstasy, they up stand up and applaud interminably.

Note

Possibly reference could be made to the episode involving Amedeo Trilli, an actor who, when playing the part of a character who was supposed to commit suicide on stage with a revolver, found to his dismay that the person who should have put the gun in the drawer of the desk had forgotten to do so.

Desperate glances in the wings, the audience waits, Trilli continues to open drawers, then he makes the heroic decision to commit suicide, come what may. But with what? By strangling himself? By beating his head on the table? Finally, the absurd yet brilliant solution: he takes off one of his boots and hits his head with it, while, in the wings, the pistol shot rings out in perfect synchronism.

The magic bedside table

ANOTHER SUGGESTION FOR THE ROLLS ROYCE
In the dark countryside, the illuminated Rolls Royce is full of beautiful girls who call the
Protagonist by name. He gets in, greedy and happy:

PROTAGONIST: Hi there, honeys! Madam. And you, haven't you worked with me before? How nice you were! What was the film? What a beautiful little face! Well girls, what are you doing here?

A GIRL: But this is one of your favorite fantasies, Signor Paolo (or Signor Marcello)! The Rolls in open country, at night, full of girls who are all happy to be with you!

PROTAGONIST: It's true, thank goodness! This fantasy is certainly better than the other one, on the train! A nightmare! By the way, do you think I've changed a lot?

THE GIRLS IN CHORUS: Oh no! You are still our nice little tubby! And the magic bedside table, how's it going, Signor Paolo (or Signor Marcello)? Does it still work?

The protagonist smiles at the audience and explains:

PROTAGONIST: Perhaps I haven't ever told you about it. It's the table beside my bed, where, since I was a kid, before going to sleep, I put whoever I wanted, sitting down or standing up. In the dark, I began to think: who do I want here, on the bedside table, this evening? My favorite guest at that time was Pamela, a buxom young peasant girl who worked for a few hours a day at our house. The bedside table was really magic, it rotated slowly, so I was able to see Pamela from the front, from the back... what a lot of women I put on it! Famous movie stars, the pharmacist's wife, and, what's her name... Zanarini's cashier. I even put a tray of pastries in her hands. Once my mother suddenly arrived with the priest. "Well," she said, "what's going on here?"

A question that the protagonist could well ask the girls in the Rolls Royce is:

PROTAGONIST: What film would you like to see me in, what role?

Suggestions by the beautiful girls, and appearances by the protagonist in the parts proposed.

*(Professor Unrat? Yes—but he falls in love, he
loses his heart to a transvestite.)*

Brief note
*When the protagonist irritably bumps into her,
the seamstress of the company asks resentfully,
"Did you get out of bed on the wrong side this
morning?" Then, smiling indulgently, she says,
"Aren't I on the bedside table any more?"*

Other probable themes

1) The C.A.T
In the great magnetic resonance tube, the
voices of the doctors are heard through loud-
speakers: "Breathe deeply, hold your breath,
breathe out."

2) The mirror
In the dressing-room. In the bathroom. At
the barber's. All the reflecting surfaces send
him an image over which he has no control.

3) Insomnia
The two Korean princesses, mother and
daughter.

4) The diets
The refrigerator
At night, irresistible temptation.

5) The probable "if's"
Where will they continue their lives, and
how? An imaginary journey to visit them, to
find out how they have lived out or are living
out their probable existences.

A film about Venice "is an enterprise that cannot succeed because it attempts to describe the indescribable," that is to say, a city which is "a theatrical invention, a figment of the imagination, a dream." But Fellini had planned it for a long time: since well before September 1992 (when an outline was completed), at least since 1975–76, when he made *Casanova*; and he had discussed it with his Venetian friends Andrea Zanzotto, a poet, Carlo Della Corte, a writer, and Tiziano Risso, who all made suggestions and offered assistance. He wrote the story-line as if it were a film or part of a television series for the RAI, *Block-notes di un regista (A Director's Notebook)*.

Besides literary evocations of Venice—imaginative and problematic—the unpublished text bears satirical witness to Fellini's hostility to Italian commercial television and its main exponent, Silvio Berlusconi, who is described buying up the whole city and invading "the Grand Canal, renamed Canale Cinque" (one of Berlusconi's television channels).

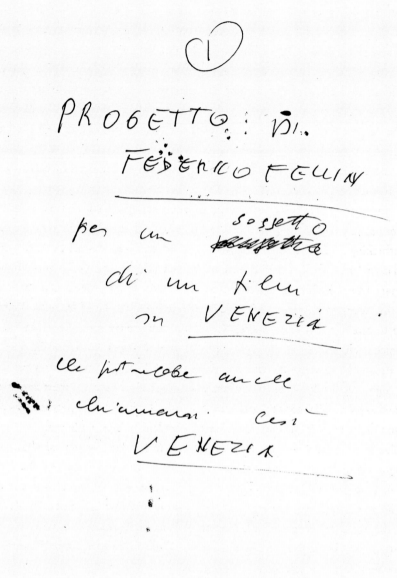

PROJECT BY FEDERICO FELLINI:
for the story-line of a film about VENICE which could also be called: this is VENICE
F. Fellini

A film about Venice? Why? First of all because I have been mulling over the idea for a long time, and then because it offers fascinating figurative and pictorial seductions, very congenial to my approach to the cinema, or rather the cinematographic mode of story-telling. In other words, it is a series of tesserae, as in a mosaic, that separate and disintegrate the story, the situations, and the characters, in a molecular decomposition continually threatened by further fragmentation. In this the mirage of unity also reverberates, with a vision and a panorama of a city that seems to be even more breathtaking because it is mirrored in the water and is vibrant with light and reflections.

But apart from all this, in a few words, what are the narrative elements that have induced me to attempt this undertaking? Certainly Venice itself, chosen as the representation of a dreamlike dimension, with its ever changing light and color, the marvelously materialized expression of an artistic dream, a nonhuman vista, a truly magic city threatened by annihilation, by disappearance, something that perhaps will no longer exist in the future, just as it may never have existed.

Well, let's see: Venice, all right, the light, the color, the sounds, the fog, the reflection of the sun, the snow, the palaces, the canals, the lagoon in the winter, the islands... All right, it's all very beautiful, all extraordinary, all well worth describing, it's all a spectacle, magic, charm, a fairy tale, but then what? What happens next? What are the basic elements of the story and who are the characters?

In a vague, confused, contradictory attempt to identify a narrative outline for the project for a film that claims to represent the city of Venice, I shall try to suggest, in an interchangeable order, a series of motifs, pretexts, images, and stories that could constitute the chapters. Thus, to give the story continuity, contrast, and tone that may simply be chromatic, or because they have been suggested by a flashback, an imaginative hypothesis, or a historical reconstruction, the chapters could suggest the structure of a free narrative in the film, which, like a fairy tale, would be liberated from time and logic. This is how Venice appears to me. Before I forget, I would like to describe two images that could give a fantastic impression of the city seen from above.

a) From a plane. An indecipherable alphabet of signs or hieroglyphics, recalling the Sumerian ones, creates a mysterious map, a tapestry, an interminable decorative motif that extends for hundreds of kilometers, creating whimsical, arabesqued arms of sea water that enter the land, spreading out in thousands of winding canals, riverlets, and pools that, from above, look like an immense Persian carpet.

b) Remember also the other image of very small white cirrus clouds like pieces of cotton wool floating far away below the plane; bathed in sunlight, they cast their shadows, like myriads of minute black-petalled flowers, onto the leaden surface of the sea.

Many years ago I read a story by Poe, just a few pages, but nobody else had ever managed to represent so marvelously the melancholy, surreal fascination of the city of Venice. Well, I shall now transcribe the story that, I think, is called *The Assignation*. Listen.

Poe's Story

"It was a night of unusual gloom. The great clock of the Piazza had sounded the fifth hour of the Italian evening. The square of the Campanile lay silent and deserted, and the lights in the old Ducal Palace were dying fast away. I was returning home from the Piazzetta, by way of the Grand Canal. But as my gondola arrived opposite the mouth of the canal San Marco, a female voice from its recesses broke suddenly upon the night, in one wild, hysterical, and long-continued shriek. Startled at the sound, I sprang upon my feet; while the gondolier, letting slip his single oar, lost it in the pitchy darkness beyond a chance of recovery, and we were consequently left to the guidance of the current which here sets from the greater into the smaller channel. Like some huge and sable-feathered condor, we were slowly drifting down toward the Bridge of Sighs, when a thousand flambeaux flashing from the windows, and down the staircases of the Ducal Palace, turned all at once that deep gloom into a livid and preternatural day.

A child, slipping from the arms of its own mother, had fallen from an upper window of the lofty structure into the deep and dim canal. The quiet waters had closed placidly over their victim; and, although my own gondola was the only one in sight, many a stout swimmer, already in the stream, was seeking in vain upon the surface, the treasure which was to be found, alas! only within the abyss. Upon the broad black marble flagstones at the entrance of the palace, and a few steps above the water, stood a figure which none who then saw can have ever since forgotten. It was the Marchesa Aphrodite—the adoration of all Venice—the gayest of the gay—the most lovely where all were beautiful—but still the young wife of the old and intriguing Mentoni, and the mother of that fair child, her first and only one, who now, deep beneath the murky water, was thinking in bitterness of heart upon her sweet caresses, and exhausting its little life in struggles to call upon her name.

She stood alone. Her small, bare and silvery feet gleamed in the black mirror of marble beneath her. Her hair, not as yet more than half loosened for the night from its ball-room array, clustered, amid a shower of diamonds, round and round her classical head, in curls like those of the young hyacinth. A snowy-white and gauze-like drapery seemed to be nearly the sole covering to her delicate form; but the mid-summer and midnight air was hot, sullen, and still, and no motion in the statue-like form itself, stirred even the folds of that raiment of very vapor which hung around it as the heavy marble hangs around the Niobe. Yet—strange to say!—her large lustrous eyes were not turned downward upon that grave wherein her brightest hope lay buried—but riveted in a widely different direction! The prison of the Old Republic is, I think, the stateliest building in all Venice—but how could that lady gaze so fixedly upon it, when beneath her lay stifling her own child? Yon dark, gloomy niche, too, yawns right opposite her chamber window—what, then, *could* there be in its shadows—in its architecture—in its ivy-wreathed and solemn cornices—that the Marchesa di Mentoni had not wondered at a thousand times before? Nonsense!—Who does not remember that, at such a time as this, the eye, like a shattered mirror, multiplies the images of its sorrow, and sees in innumerable far-off places, the woe which is close at hand?

Many steps above the Marchesa, and within the arch of the water-gate, stood, in full dress, the Satyr-like figure of Mentoni himself. He was occasionally occupied in thrumming a guitar, and seemed *ennuyé* to the very death, as at intervals he gave directions for the recovery of his child. Stupefied and aghast, I had myself no power to move from the upright position I had assumed upon first hearing the shriek, and must have presented to the eyes of the agitated group a spectral and ominous appearance, as with pale countenance and rigid limbs, I floated down among them in that funereal gondola. All efforts proved in vain. Many of the most energetic in the search were relaxing their exertions, and yielding to a gloomy sorrow. There seemed to be little hope for the child; (how much less than for the mother!) but now, from the interior of that dark niche which has already been mentioned as forming part of the Old Republican prison, and as fronting the lattice of the Marchesa, a figure muffled in a cloak, stepped out within reach of the light, and, pausing a moment upon the verge of the giddy descent, plunged headlong into the canal. As, in an instant afterward, he stood with the still living and breathing child within his grasp, upon the marble flagstones by the side of the Marchesa, his cloak, heavy with the drenching water, became unfastened, and, falling in folds about his feet, discovered to the wonder-stricken spectators the graceful person of a very young man, with the sound of whose name the greater part of Europe was then ringing.

No word spoke the deliverer. But the Marchesa! She will now receive her child—she will press it to her heart—she will cling to its little form, and smother it with her caresses. Alas! *another's* arms have taken it from the stranger—*another's* arms have taken it away, and borne it afar off, unnoticed, into the palace! And the Marchesa! Her lip—her beautiful lip trembles; tears are gathering in her eyes—those eyes which, like Pliny's acanthus, are "soft and almost liquid." Yes! tears are gathering in those eyes—and see! the entire woman thrills throughout the soul, and the statue has started into life! The pallor of the marble countenance, the swelling of the marble bosom, the very purity of the marble feet, we behold suddenly flushed over with a tide of ungovernable crimson; and a slight shudder quivers about her delicate frame, as a gentle air at Naples about the rich silver lilies in the grass.

Why *should* that lady blush! To this demand there is no answer—except that, having left, in the eager haste and terror of a mother's heart, the privacy of her own *boudoir*, she has neglected to enthral her tiny feet in their slippers, and utterly forgotten to throw over her Venetian shoulders that drapery which is their due. What other possible reason could there have been for her so blushing?—for the glance of those wild appealing eyes?—for the unusual tumult of that throbbing bosom?—for the convulsive pressure of that trembling hand?—that hand which fell as Mentoni turned into the palace, accidentally, upon the hand of the

stranger. What reason could there have been for the low—the singularly low tone of those unmeaning words which the lady uttered hurriedly in bidding him adieu? "Thou hast conquered," she said, or the murmurs of the water deceived me; "thou hast conquered—one hour after sunrise—we shall meet—so let it be!"
This is the end of Poe's story, or rather of the part that interests me with regard to my film about Venice.

How is it possible to describe in a more stimulating and fascinating way, and with great expressive power, the sense of unreality, magic, and mystery with which Venice overwhelms you, making you quite helpless in your attempt to discover its secret? This could be the problem that torments the director who for some time has dreamed of making a film about Venice. I do not know whether the director should be an Italian, but perhaps it would be better to choose as the character who persists with this idea an American director: let us imagine an aging director who loves Europe; in other words, he is a sensitive person who is familiar with our classics.

He visited Venice for the first time many years before when he was on his honeymoon; or else (and maybe this would be better) during his first visit he met a very beautiful girl with whom he had a brief, intense love affair, after which he never heard from her again. Well, perhaps there were a few short letters over the years, but they became more and more infrequent and then there was silence. Now he wants to look for her and meet her again, but he has only vague clues as to her whereabouts, so that, as he wanders around the city, he feels increasingly discouraged and uncertain, and he is continually disappointed.

I want to note as an image the fantastic apparition in a very narrow, dark canal that I was crossing in a gondola, looking for a friend who had invited me to dinner; the houses loomed up like the sides of a canyon, and the total silence was broken only by the lapping of the water against the side of the funereal boat and the warning cry of the gondolier as we were about to turn, brushing against the crumbling walls, into another canal that was even darker and more foul smelling. Suddenly, a few hundred meters ahead in the deep gloom of the canal, we saw a small light, like the flame of a candle, shining on the surface of the water. Despite the distance, we could hear low voices, and, as we approached this sort of will-o'-the-wisp, we saw that the flame was burning in a saucer placed in the middle of a rubber dinghy, the dark color of which was very similar to that of the water; in it there were two young people who, stark naked, embraced each other and spoke quietly, looking up at the narrow strip of sky that could be glimpsed beyond the black edges of the roofs.

I have noted down this recollection because it could form part of the quest of the elderly director as he wanders around the city. In this quest of his he could be accompanied by a Venetian or Milanese noblewoman, or one who lives in Treviso in a splendid villa that is also haunted by illustrious ghosts. Together with some friends of hers, this noblewoman has been given the task of preparing a very refined meal, using the recipes of the Gonzaga; this forms part of the festivities being organized for the inauguration of a carnival based on a futuristic or historical theme.

The motif of the preparation of a banquet could also be used as a narrative thread leading to various characters in their patrician houses, the villas of the mainland, or the large hotels of the Lido frequented by fashionable people: artists, adventurers, intermediaries, show-business celebrities, famous actresses, fashion models, fags, male prostitutes, corrupt and decadent Americans, secret agents, and politicians.

Another fascinating and mysterious place is Harry's Bar, the favorite haunt of the international jet set and the Venetian aristocracy;

here you can find everything, from sheiks, drug peddlers, high-class whores to would-be writers from abroad in search of inspiration.

Another fascinating theme, which is also distressing because it is almost inexplicable, concerns the hordes—the processions, the veritable armies—of tourists, who, dressed in the strangest of attires, often half-naked and in shorts, leaving wrappings, cans, and excrement everywhere amidst the fantastic stage sets of the magic city, surge interminably along the canals and alleys, and over the bridges, parading endlessly behind someone holding up a sign on a stick or a handkerchief.... But where are they going? Where on earth are all these people going? What have they come to see? What are they looking for? Where do they go at night? Where do they sleep? Under the water maybe? Who knows, it might be possible to see, in the moonlight, a crowd of tourists who, like shoals of salmon standing up, move under the surface.... In any case, hallucinatory as it may be, in my opinion, the theme of the tourists represents very disturbing, grotesque material for a narrative, just as the interminable rows of shop windows and restaurants at the Mercerie appear to be bizarre or even spectral: windows with macabre mannequins that seem to have been hanged. I remember one at the end of an alley: when you approached it, a hidden photoelectric cell slowly lit it up and two headless men in tuxedos appeared; when you got closer the light suddenly went out, and now only the heads were illuminated, without the bodies.

Now, we follow this dirty, sweaty throng, speaking their unknown, guttural, incomprehensible languages, ice creams in their hands and rope-soled sandals on their feet, as they wander around the churches and museums; all around them, the mysterious, sublime paintings by Tiepolo, Titian, Veronese, and Correggio seem to dissolve and disappear, move away and vanish. Another theme that I think could constitute a third or fourth narrative thread is the growing threat caused by the crumbling of various palaces, which risk being swallowed up by the canals. This catastrophe has been foreseen for some time now, but no one seems to pay much attention to it. Every attempt to deal with this situation has come to nothing. In the archives there are hundreds of plans: one morning, accompanied by a couple of professors and the archivist, we pay a visit to the former monastery that now houses the State Archives.

Only that night another old palace has slipped into the lagoon. We watch the collapse, the slow disappearance of the splendid facade of the palace, which slides into the murky waters and disappears. Surrounded by boats and the bathyspheres of the team of experts under the command of a Dutch hydraulic engineer sent by the government to devise desperate systems for saving the city, which is in ever-increasing danger of disappearing into the lagoon. In this apocalyptic atmosphere, threatened by the sea, Venice, as in the *Masque of the Red Death* by Poe, attempts to forget the nightmare of the disaster by organizing festivities. We follow the preparations for the fantastic carnival as the costumes are made ready in the immense buildings of the Corderie (rope-walk) at the Arsenale (the naval dockyard), with the Admiral—since the Arsenale is a naval area—who insists on showing the director and his retinue the military structures of the Venetian Republic before Napoleon (the thief!) so vilely defeated it.

Meanwhile, the king of private television (Silvio Berlusconi) is buying up nearly all of Venice: he buys the Arsenale, Santa Maria della Salute, the most magnificent palaces, and the main hotels. It is all his, and he wants to build a Bucintoro (the doge's state barge) and cross the Grand Canal, renamed Canale Cinque (one of his television channels). In Venice he has assembled all his managers, advisers, agents, and public relations people, all gathered together to welcome him. He arrives in a helicopter, bringing as a prize the latest creature of his show-business empire, a splendid girl (a second fundamental female protagonist of the film), who could be Lorella Cuccarini. When she was very young, she rose rapidly to fame by advertising on TV the sanitary ware of a provincial firm, which, thanks to her image, increased its turnover tenfold. For this reason, the girl is paid staggering sums, and all the salesmen of the industry take part in the convention, enthusiastic and jubilant in the presence of the boss. There is also the director of the ad spots, an ambitious young man, humiliated and bitter, who is asked to illustrate the campaign to the sales force.

But other helicopters are slowly circling in the sky, wary and menacing. They are military aircraft, which, together with motorboats and, presumably, submarines, are watching over the security of the conference of the seven leading industrial powers that is taking place at Torcello.

All this is being televised by the network of the new owner of Venice: the summit of the politicians; the collapse of the palace; the bathtubs in the form of gondolas intended to launch new articles of sanitary ware with the gondolier girl. Meanwhile, like a reincarnation of Captain Nemo, the Dutch engineer in his bathysphere fitted with the most sophisticated equipment for underwater observation, travels day and night through the mysterious foundations of the city. In the powerful lights of his little submarine and those of his divers—the explorers of a submerged land—appears an underwater landscape with its unimaginable vistas that seem to be the setting for a science-fiction story. It consists of a boundless labyrinth of piles, rising amidst huge, crumbling foundations and immense ruins of sunken palaces, where millions of rats and spectral marine animals live in the miry gloom that, every now and again, vibrates as boats pass overhead.

This engineer could be accompanied by a

64

beautiful woman that he intends to marry, or else he could meet a Venetian noblewoman with a regal bearing who asks if she can go with him during his fascinating, frightening submersions. Either of them, however, would have to reveal an aspect of her character that is completely unsuspected by everyone, maybe hidden even from herself. Fantasies, desires, habits, and the need for mysterious, awe-inspiring femininity are revealed by mythological creatures, just as Venice, in the depths of its drained canals, reveals an unimaginable substratum composed of putrefied layers.

In this story, I would also like to have a small group of restorers who, with their devoted, patient work, are busy saving masterpieces of the past threatened by inexorable decay. The young woman in charge of the group is a painter, who is sustained in her task by mystic fervor; naturally she must be good-looking, very cultured and intelligent, and she has the charm and freshness of an adolescent.

And to all these stories that are intermingled with each other, I would like to add this one by Schiller. Now do not ask me how it will fit into the film: it is perfectly suitable, and it will be very easy to find a pretext for inserting it at some point. Here is the story:

The following evening we met in Piazza San Marco earlier than usual. A sudden downpour obliged us to enter a cafe where people were gambling. The Prince stood behind the chair of a Spaniard and watched the game. I went into an adjacent room to read the newspapers. Not long after this, I heard an uproar. Before the Prince arrived, the Spaniard was in a losing streak; now, all his cards were winning ones. The fortunes of the game had been sensationally reversed, and the bank ran the risk of breaking due to the stakes of the Spaniard, who was emboldened by the favorable turn that his luck had taken. The Venetian who kept the bank rudely told the Prince to go away from the table because he was disturbing

the course of fortune. The Prince looked at him coldly and did not move; he remained impassive when the Venetian repeated his affront in French. Thinking that the Prince did not understand either language, the Venetian addressed the others with a scornful laugh: "Tell me, gentlemen, how can I make this dullard understand me?" At the same time he stood up and attempted to seize the Prince by the arm; at this point the latter lost his patience and, taking hold of the Venetian, threw him roughly to the ground. The whole cafe was now in turmoil. Hearing the noise, I rushed into the room and unwittingly called out: "Be careful, Prince," adding imprudently, "we are in Venice." At the mention of the Prince's name, a hush fell, followed by a murmur that seemed dangerous to me. All the Italians present formed a group together; one after the other they left the room, until we were left alone with the Spaniard and a number of Frenchmen. "Gracious Sir," said they, "you are lost if you do not leave the city immediately. The Venetian that you have treated so badly is rich and influential, and it would cost him only fifty sequins to have you killed." The Spaniard offered to obtain bodyguards to accompany the Prince to his home. The Frenchmen offered to do the same. We were still pondering over what to do, when the door opened and a number of officers of the State Inquisition entered. They showed us a warrant issued by the Seigniory that ordered us to go with them immediately. With a large escort, they took us to the Canal. Here a gondola awaited us, and we had to sit in it. Before disembarking, they blindfolded us. We were led up a large stone staircase and then along a tortuous corridor that, at one point, passed over an arch, judging by the echoes that reverberated under our feet. Finally we reached another staircase that descended with twenty-six steps. We found ourselves in the middle of a circle of venerable elders, all dressed in black;

the whole room was draped with black cloths and illuminated by a weak light; the total silence that reigned over the whole assembly was extremely frightening. One of these old men, probably the head of the State Inquisitors, approached the Prince and, as he led him before the Venetian, asked him with a solemn air: "Is this the man who offended you in the cafe?" "Yes," replied the Prince. After this, the old man addressed the prisoner. "Is this the person that you wanted to kill this evening?" The prisoner replied in the affirmative.

Immediately the circle opened up and, to our great horror, we saw that the Venetian's head was cut clean from his body. "Are you satisfied with this punishment?" asked the State Inquisitor. But the Prince had fainted into the arms of his escort. "Now be gone," continued the Inquisitor with his dreadful voice, addressing me, "and in future be less hasty in your judgment of Venetian justice."

In my opinion, this story by Schiller, like the preceding ones by Poe, increases our expectations—and our trepidation—in a way that is very congenial to the project. They are a mirror for the mystery that is being evoked and, at the same time, they constitute raw material, narrative islands where we can tie up during our wanderings through the enchanted and elusive city. Thus, the stories by Poe and Schiller become encounters with the lagoon, just like the episodes with the hydraulic engineer's bathysphere or the convention with Lorella Cuccarini. I believe that the novelty of the proposal hinges on this apparent lack of homogeneity, almost as if the story is intended to take the same form as the lagoon, an equilibrium between land and sea, between voids and solids; that is, indeed, also the play that characterizes Venetian architecture, its disquieting and delicate style, its treacherous yet pleasing tracery. The interplay of light and shade, a tale that is visionary, fantastic, and stratified, part in costume, part present-day, and part invented, as if the very limits of time and space were dissolved in the single liquid element on which Venice floats, and everything exists together in a single, inviolable mystery.

Perhaps the key to the film, its basic idea, its underlying sentiment, could be the futility, the insurmountable difficulty, the impossibility, the utter absurdity of trying to describe in a manner more appropriate to the theater—scenically, that is—pictorial references, metaphorical processes, ethereal effects, and the oneiric fascination of a city—Venice—that appears to be, expresses itself as, indeed is a theatrical invention, a figment of the imagination, a dream.

With its continual changing, this interplay of mirrors—in its attempt to reflect and capture an image that already appears as the reflection of something else—becomes, in effect, deceitful, and gives the ambitious film director a sense of defeat. He cannot succeed, he gives up, he succumbs. It is the story of an enterprise that cannot succeed because it attempts to describe the indescribable, in other words, to give material form to a city that does not exist, because it is built on water and painted in the air. However, the real Venice will always seem to be more metaphorical, mysterious, spectral, and oneiric than the city that the director will attempt to portray in his film.

This is the project that I am proposing, and, once someone shows interest in it, I can start work by concentrating on the literary part—this seems to me the most fruitful system—making notes, adding new characters, outlining dialogues and, possibly, at this stage, being fortunate enough to invent new episodes. But this phase cannot be separated from the other one, which is even more important for me, in other words the actual preparation of the film: the sets, the costumes, the faces, on-the-spot inspections, and experiments with models of everything that has to be done in the studio. However, we shall see.

66

68

Drawing for the makeup
artist Otello Fava
indicating how to prepare
Marcello Mastroianni
for *La Dolce Vita*

72

The Inferno of the *Divine Comedy* becomes the hell experienced by Fellini when he was besieged by American and (perhaps) Japanese television producers who wanted the leading Italian director to make a film version of Dante Alighieri's famous work. He received numerous proposals of this kind over the years: Fellini describes his own comical vicissitudes, himself, reluctant and bewildered, impersonated by a puppet. The *Inferno* was intended to be one of the television specials in the series *Block-notes di un regista* for the RAI, the Italian public television network.

The unpublished text, a comic parody, quotes the French critic and scholar Jacqueline Risset, who translated the *Divine Comedy* into her own language. It draws on the director's autobiography in the reminiscences of his school days. It refers to a visit to the mental hospital at Maggiano, near Lucca, which Fellini made around 1955, guided by his doctor and writer friend Mario Tobino, who at the time was director of this institution; and also to Fellini's experience of taking LSD in the early sixties, in the presence of two doctors, a chemist, two nurses, a stenographer, and lots of microphones.

Series: *Block-notes di un regista* by Federico
Fellini

Provisional script for *Block-notes no. 5*

N.B. This draft is intended, above all, to help
the production staff to make a rough estimate
of the costs (constructions, characters) and to
calculate the shooting time.

Another aim of the story-line in the script
presented here is to suggest the narrative
structure for a more detailed screenplay,
which I intend to write sooner or later.

How many times has it been suggested, in extremely insistent ways, that I make a film of the *Divine Comedy*?

"It's an obligation that you have, a duty!" said one of the CBS lawyers, who was sucking on huge cigars as if they were lollipops, at a certain point during one of many meetings. (Where were we? At the Grand Hotel? In Venice? In Cannes? In London?)

For many years now I have been pursued, courted, threatened by these strange would-be backers.

"You can't refuse, you're Italian, Dante's Italian, the Americans admire you—though I have to admit that I haven't understood all of your movies."

"You're a legend," said the woman who was interpreting, while the lawyer with the big cigar, looking at me in a somewhat hostile manner, hastily concluded by stating that it was his duty to explain to the Americans just what Dante was going to do in Hell.

"Mr. President, Athens calling." The secretary passed the phone to the tall thin man in shirtsleeves wearing suspenders, who immediately started talking Greek. We all kept quiet, without understanding a word. The other lawyer (Mexican? he was very dark-skinned, anyhow) signaled to me to pay attention, and with slow gestures that were both solemn and conspiratorial began to unroll a large poster depicting an enormous truck tire with a wedding veil streaming in the wind and a garland of orange blossoms placed above it.

"Two million dollars! Just Firestone and P. & Company Wedding Dresses. And this is only the start. The sponsors are lining up for this project! Mr. Fellini, what's wrong? Why are you playing hard to get?"

But I wasn't playing hard to get, even though this was the fifth time that I had met presidents, vice presidents, sponsors, lawyers... and always in hotel suites, in the midst of a whirl of waiters, trays with silver lids, turkeys, sole, liqueurs, clouds of smoke, phones ringing first in one room and then in the others, the names of cities and continents being shouted out, while there is continuous knocking at the door and other personages enter: close relatives of the Mexican, Sicilians who had helped the Americans in the landings during the Second World War, kisses, hugs, mozzarella cheese from Anversa, boxes full of photographs of actors that are scattered on the sofas, on the floor... a babel of tongues: English, French, Spanish, Armenian....

"Thirty-three episodes!" And they thrust three splayed fingers into my face. All the television networks in the world offer a "terrific" guaranteed minimum! For my part, on various occasions I had raised what I thought were quite reasonable objections, but they did not believe me, and I had to listen to the figures of enormous takings, recitals of famous tercets, and endless lists of awards received.

The Mexican lawyer asked me to look at his eyes; they filled with tears as he murmured just one line—only one!: "era già l'ora che volge al disio...."

Bewildered, confused, and alienated, I sprawled motionless in the armchair, a glass of champagne in my hand: "A puppet, I was just a puppet...."

It is at this point, while my voice is saying this, that two workmen, who have been hovering in a corner as if they were waiting for a signal, carrying a mannequin wearing an overcoat and a scarf, could say: "Shall we put it here, sir?"

Following my affirmative reply, they come onto the set and place the Fellini puppet in the armchair, putting the glass in his hand. (I believe that this is the best solution to the problem of the director's presence in the film. I do not feel like playing myself; I could avoid letting the character be seen, but I think this is an old trick that would make the sacred invisibility of the director seem merely to be a pretext, or even presumptuous. A puppet, on the other hand, would be able to express the sense of helplessness, of not belonging, of alienation felt by the director when faced with the truly infernal procession of faces, places, and situations that are increasingly confusing as no efforts are spared in the attempt to oblige the puppet to accept the project.)

In the scene I have just outlined, everyone will continue to address the immobile simulacrum, which will, from time to time, reply with my voice; or else, eyeless and mouthless, it will imperturbably express my thoughts.

"Do you know who I was speaking to on the phone, Mr. Fellini? To the greatest composer of film music that I have ever had the good fortune to meet. Do you agree?"

Seeing my embarrassment, the speaker gave the secretary a withering glance; looking hard at me, she immediately replied that she had sent me three cassettes, twice over!

And while the puppet declares that he intends to listen carefully to them that very evening, I try to think where I might have put them. Generally speaking, I gave all my scripts, cassettes, LPs and CDs to Teresa, a fabulous large-bottomed woman whom I was particularly fond of at the time.

Here she is, Big Bottom, kneeling down and rummaging in the fireplace and a case. There is also a friend of Big Bottom's, an intellectual lady photographer in boots, rather like Elisabetta Catalano, who, squeezing the end of her nose between her thumb and forefinger, declares polemically that this time she would not make the mistake of shooting everything at Cinecittà; she would shoot it on location, seeking villages, cities, and other places that were really infernal. The idea of

journeys, unknown cities, and big hotels makes the large-bottomed female sit up and listen with delight as her friend talks about the Amazon ("Why do you...?"), India, Calcutta, Benares.... Big Bottom mentions belly-dancing, while the other speaks about Greenland and the North Pole.... "What a change from Fregene and Ostia (towns on the coast near Rome)!" the former exclaims cheerfully. Then, with a shout, she announces that she has finally found the cassette of Greek music. There is silence. We listen to the music, in which the composer attempts to conjure up imposing, terrifying images of Dante's *Inferno*. But we hardly hear anything, just the hiss of the tape, then a sort of hiccup, then the hiss once again. Big Bottom fiddles with the cassette, suspecting she may have put it in the wrong way. We settle down to listen once more, but the only noise that comes out of the recorder now is a strangled gasping, then the sound of a whistle. This is really modern music, ultra-twelve-note: in comparison, Stockhausen sounds like Puccini.

Catalano is very annoyed. Big Bottom is fantasizing about the wonderful journeys she could go on with the puppet, providing, of course, he agrees to make the film of the *Inferno*.

And the puppet? What does he think? He's thinking about Jacqueline Risset, whom he is going to see tomorrow at the University. The famous Dantean scholar has arranged to meet him in the students' canteen.

It is the following day: here is the meeting with Jacqueline, who talks fervently about Dante, and the ethical and poetic tenets that are the basis of a venture that can on no account be rejected.

"Only you can do it!" she tells the puppet, who, disheartened and resigned, repeats his objections for the hundredth time.

What language do they speak? Do they recite poetry? How are they dressed? But, in my opinion, the cinema should not be mere illustration, and anyway I can't remember anything about Dante: perhaps I wasn't particularly fond of him at school. In the first place, the high school was named after Dante Alighieri; when I put up my hand to ask to go to the toilet, in the corridor as vast as the nave of a church, just outside the classroom, in a niche full of cobwebs that greatly annoyed the headmaster (but the janitor was never able to find a ladder high enough for him to clean it), on a column of gelid marble there was a black metal bust with blank, wide-open eyes. It had the severe expression of a judge—or a tattletale. In fact, we were all convinced that it was the bust, with its lips as thin as blades, that sneaked to the teachers about our misdemeanors during recess.

Some more ideas
"The devil, Charon, with eyes of glowing coals," was the old beggar, a violent, brutal drunkard who followed us with a cudgel, his beard yellowish, his eyes bloodshot. (Imagine, down in the port of Rimini, on a very foggy day, the arrival of a boat piloted by the old beggar: "Woe to you, perverted souls!" while we students greet him with a chorus of raspberries and cries of "Fuck off!")

A conference in an almost unbearably magnificent or austere hall. The subject is: "Dante and Psychoanalysis." A madman is speaking, and what he says is quite incomprehensible. But Jacqueline is even more passionate and convinced. This time she has the poet Orelli on her side; he reads Dante onomatopoeically, emitting a whole range of sounds, including grunts, labials, dentals, and gargles, that cause Jacqueline to applaud, enraptured and deeply moved.

"But don't you hear how all this resembles you, Federico?"

In effect, the puppet is beginning to give way. But the memory of the illustrations by Doré, which the Americans of another television network had strewn all along the corridors of a Paris hotel, in a final, clumsy attempt to convince him, make him feel perplexed once again.

And now, what are they doing all together, including the puppet, noses up at against the windows at the Venice airport? They are watching a plane coming from London that will land in a few minutes; on board is a famous English actor—a star, a box-office success with his latest films.

The aircraft lands, the photographers rush toward a young fair-haired man who is the first to come down the steps, followed by other men and women. "Fair he was, and beautiful...," quotes one of the group approaching the actor.

"So young?!" thinks the puppet, "he doesn't even remotely resemble the black head at my high school." Here they are, all in the motorboat, on their way to the hotel at the Lido, where the new television executives, sponsors, secretaries, lawyers, and interpreters have organized a symposium in order to make a massive attack on, and hopefully overcome, the puppet's unjustifiable, unendurable objections. He has a hallucinatory vision: beyond the foam-topped waves formed by the motorboat's prow, he sees hideous devils with bat's wings perched on the solitary posts that protrude here and there from the surface of the lagoon. One of these, wearing spectacles on his hooked nose, calls out his name, flapping his awful wings as a salutation.

"Hello Federico, do you remember me? I'm Piacentini from Modena."

"Yes, I do," thinks the puppet. Piacentini from Modena. He was the unpleasant colleague on the newspaper where the puppet used to work.

He makes the rude gesture of placing his right hand in the crook of his left arm; and the devil "blew back with his bugle of an ass-hole."

Showing of a film of Dante's *Inferno*, made in 1910, amid great applause.

In a last attempt to find a way of representing the horrors of Hell with less traditional visual images, the puppet remembers his visit to the mental hospital at Maggiano: the cells, the mad monk in an uncontrollable fit of sexual excitement. ("He jerks off fifty times a day!" says one of the nurses, and they grab hold of him, one on each side, by his wrists, as he rushes out of the dark and stench of his cell, naked, dripping with sweat, his enormous member erect as a sword and his tongue darting back and forth like that of a snake.)

And the man who was convinced that he was Saint Peter, emanating a profound sense of peace and indescribable serenity.

Another dinner. Where are we this time? In a hotel once more, or in a trattoria in Trastevere? The director-puppet recounts his experience with LSD: he describes the horror of the forms that surround us and the fact that we no longer remember their significance, their meaning, their function, what they are. They are scattered, without consciousness, memories, yearning, regrets, or hopes in meaningless immensity. This is Hell and, at the same time, the horror of the mortal unknownness of everything suddenly radiates you with boundless happiness, freedom that goes beyond all the universes: you are no longer a prisoner of meanings and concepts, you are no longer separated from objects, from others, from the reality that is external to you, but you yourself become everything: you are the flower, the sea, the eyes of that woman, the bird in the sky... you are the whole creation, the mystic rose, the center of paradise....

The puppet attempts to recount all this while, all around, everyone is eating, drinking, and laughing, and when he has finished his story an embarrassed silence falls. Perhaps for the first time the puppet has managed to convey the sense of powerlessness that assails him at the thought of making the *Inferno*.

The last scene could be shot in a studio. The actors who play the parts of Paolo and Francesca (lovers in Dante's *Inferno*) are raised by pulleys, almost to the roof, where powerful aircraft propellers agitate whirls of smoke and leaves, simulating "the infernal storm, eternal in its rage." Dante murmurs to Virgil that he would like to speak to those two, and "as doves, called by desire...." (etc.).

Then follows the episode of Paolo and Francesca, who, despite the theatrical machinery, the make-believe of the circus, the shouts, and the din of the plane engines, arouse profound emotions.

Useless notes

a) Remember that the truck tire, as it glides along the hotel corridor with the wedding veil aflutter and the orange blossoms aquiver, emits the sound of a musical box that is playing Mendelssohn's *Wedding March*.

b) Are there also a couple of Japanese who insist on high definition? (Check the equipment, the techniques, the experiments with the Mirage camera. Fichera will take care of this.)

c) Among the strongest objections raised by the puppet there is the one regarding the way Dante, Virgil, and so on, are dressed. One hears a lot about nudity: the devils were naked, as were the damned, and maybe during this meeting, which becomes increasingly animated, the producers, secretaries, sponsors, the black lawyer, and the lady translators appear stark naked, with bouncing bellies, buttocks, and boobs.

d) A visit to the Experimental Cinema Center to see a copy of the *Inferno* made in 1909 on a Moviola. Where is the Center? It would be necessary to invent the location, on a wasteland, in the midst of rubble and ruins; or depict it just as it really is, stressing its decay, emptiness, and desolation, as if the objectives for which it was set up now belong to the remote past. There is just one fanatical employee, who walks with an unsteady step and is half blind, and accompanies the visitors to the "cells." He says this word with priestly pride, and, despite his mummified appearance and his weak, hoarse voice, he says everything in an inspired, emotional tone. He seems to be revealing mysteries, precious secrets, incommunicable, esoteric truths. The "cells" are disposed along an interminable corridor; they are refrigerators, the doors of which open on rails with hideous screeches, allowing the visitor to peer into dark rooms. In these, at very low temperatures, cans containing thousands of films are piled up: we are in a polar movie cemetery. At the end of the corridor, the custodian opens a door and leads the guests into the projection room. Here, too, it is very cold: the ceiling, the walls, the arms of the seats, even the screen on the wall, are all encrusted with icicles. Jackets are distributed, and blankets to put on our knees; the lights go out and the film begins. On the copy that I have seen on the Moviola, it will be necessary to use a film printing machine, isolating the faces of Dante and Virgil from the long shots as if they were in the foreground.

Fellini's love of American comic-strip characters of the first half of the twentieth century, and his knowledge of their world, are well known. *Mandrake*, perhaps a collaboration, was written (says Pietro Notarianni) because of pressure from producer Dino De Laurentiis, who had long been after Fellini to direct a film for him, proposing the most disparate and outlandish themes. In 1972, Fellini's fondness for Mandrake had already become apparent: asked by the French edition of *Vogue* to edit the Christmas issue for that year, appropriately enough entitled *Vogue-Fellini*, the director had shown Marcello Mastroianni in the guise of Mandrake (with the same costume later donned by the actor in 1987 in *Interview*), and had had a comic strip of his adventures drawn, *Moi, Mandrake de Frosinone*.

The unpublished text introduces the character from different points of view: realistic, in melodramatic guise, in the form of a childish or oriental dream, in the key of proto-science fiction.

MOI, MANDRAKE DE FROSINONE[1]

PAR MARCELLO MASTROIANNI

Enfant, je me guettais dans la glace embuée après avoir pris mon bain dans une cuve à lessive, et, clignant des yeux, j'essayais d'adopter des expressions à la Mandrake, méphistophéliques mais sympathiques aussi. J'aurais surtout voulu être capable de faire quelques tours : par exemple, arrondir mes mollets. Mon grand tourment, en effet, a toujours été d'avoir des jambes trop maigres.

Je disposais aussi d'un Lothar : c'était ma tante Angelina, la figure enduite de cirage. Une petite fille qui habitait l'étage au-dessus était Narda. Malheureusement elle était amoureuse du fils unique d'un comte, que je n'arrivais pas, malgré tous mes efforts pour me concentrer au maximum, à faire disparaître. Ginger Rogers était aussi Narda pour moi. A vrai dire, Ginger Rogers n'avait pas grand-chose à voir avec le rôle d'une petite fiancée prévenante, mais elle me plaisait beaucoup tout de même. J'aimais aussi Joan Blondell à en mourir.

La buraliste était la Reine des Oiseaux, belle dame sans merci. C'était une femme bien en chair, aux yeux verts, plus belle que Mae West, qui me faisait frémir de volupté lorsqu'elle disait, la voix caverneuse : "Ciao, mon petit. Dis à ta mère qu'elle me doit encore deux kilos de sel !"

Mais pourquoi ne faisons-nous pas un film sur Mandrake ? J'en serai évidemment la vedette ; Oliver Reed, peint en noir, pourrait être Lothar tandis que, pour Narda, je proposerais Claudia Cardinale (je rectifie : je voulais dire Catherine Deneuve, qui est près de moi au moment où j'écris). J'ai dit à Federico je ne sais plus combien de fois : "Fais-moi faire Mandrake, nous allons nous amuser ! N'est-ce-pas, Federico ? Jette un coup d'œil sur la page à côté, tu verras quel serait mon premier tour."

(traduit par Ornella Volta)

M.M.

(1) Petite ville entre Rome et Naples, où est né Marcello Mastroianni.

Introduction

Mandrake was born in the summer of 1941; as a character, of course. He came onto the scene accompanied—indeed, preceeded—by the huge Black character named Lothar, who was a perfect match for him: as wild as Mandrake was genteel, as ignorant as Mandrake was cultured, as brutal as Mandrake was decadent, and all brawn, just as Mandrake was all brain. This antithesis formed an inseparable pair, an alliance that could have had homosexual overtones were it not for the complete absence of sex in the comic strips of that time. Their world was the pre-sexual one of fables; their relationship had the solid purity of the one between Ishmael and Queequeg in *Moby Dick*.

The complementary element making up the Three, the perfect number, was Narda—a pretty brunette who recalled Hedy Lamarr or Paulette Goddard—princess of a mysterious Central European principality (let us not forget that we are in the age of operettas set in Ruritania and Kurland), whom Mandrake helped and rescued several times, and who became his constant companion (although not even a kiss ever passed between them). This ever victorious trio weathered various adventures and various places, since Mandrake, unlike almost all the other comic-strip heros who have fixed abodes, ranged through Africa and Asia, between adventures and the past, through the Europe of the grand hotels and the stellar universes, thus taking on a very heterogeneous set of enemies: swindlers, gangsters, wizards, tyrants, endless monsters.

Mandrake defeated any enemy thanks to his paranormal powers—telepathy, hypnosis, illusionism, ability to make himself invisible, etc.—an acceptable magic, even if outlandish. In the first episodes, Mandrake wrought veritable miracles, that is, utterly supernatural phenomena: turning men into pieces of wood, flying, and so forth. Then, the authors realized that to give credibility and a plot to the adventures (a man with unlimited powers cannot have adventures; he is omnipotent), they had to diminish the means available to Mandrake; they left him only with exceptional powers of illusionism.

Mandrake's stories were an instant and enduring success; one might say that Mandrake is one of the few great "survivors" of American comics of the thirties. His traditional costume (blue tailcoat with top hat and cape) has recently been brought up-to-date, and in some modern comic strips he appears in normal attire, or even in a bathing suit, just as Lothar occasionally wears a white shirt and shorts instead of his old leopard-skin loincloth; but in the hearts and minds of his readers, Mandrake is unchangeable; in his get-up as illusionist of the grand hotels, he has a prewar aura about him and his fascination is that of a happy, lost world.

A worldly, bourgeois hero (certainly right wing), Mandrake enchants children because he extends into life one of his boundless magic shows, thus imbuing everything with the scent and the enchantment of the stage, clever tricks, vaudeville, an omnipotence obtained with theatrical methods (deep down, the reader-child thinks that with the help of some magic box and a little practice even he could do what Mandrake does). Add to this the specific medium of the comic strip, which by its very nature gives form and fixity to the characters-masks, and which, with the nervous lines of the drawing and clear colors, contributes to creating the graphic splendor of posters for fairs and playbills.

Fixity, form, "masks," a paper world. Mandrake and his friends and enemies alike are all two-dimensional; they have neither depth nor soul, and not even a precise birth (we are informed in passing that Lothar is an African prince in exile and that Mandrake as a child was educated in a Tibetan monastery: very little to go on), so one must accept them in all their marionette-like essentiality and not attempt to penetrate the mystery of their origins.

Film Possibilities

Looking at this material with an eye to making a film, a number of solutions come to mind.

First solution: Realism. One could follow the course of tracing Mandrake back to the figures that inspired him in order to give a realistic substance to the whole. That is, seeking the sources, the prototypes behind the character Mandrake—for example, a famous illusionist like Houdini—and telling his story, filling it out with inventions and adventures, plunging it into the fantastic atmosphere of the comic strip, but keeping at the base a concrete personality from which to draw one's inspiration. We name Houdini for convenience, but of course it should be about a nonhistorical figure; Houdini is just a point of reference.

In this case, we will find real settings at our disposal (the theater, the grand hotels, ocean liners) and an entire international world of impresarios, adventurers, actresses, and so forth, which offers a point of departure for stories built around a great illusionist who puts his exceptional powers at the service of Goodness and Honesty. This would solve the problem of the excessive "flatness" of the character Mandrake, as we would take our inspiration not so much from him as from his archetype, living in a distinct historical period.

Second solution: the Operetta. This is, so to speak, an opposite solution: in fact, it would accentuate the fantastic, fake side, ironically conventional in many of Mandrake's stories. Indeed, there is in Mandrake (especially in

the episodes with Narda and her brother Prince Siegrid) a strong sense of that Hungarian, Central European atmosphere found in *The Prisoner of Zenda*, which was in vogue in the thirties; and this film about Mandrake would lend itself to constructing a magnificent and enthralling operetta (not musical, of course) set in a Grand Duchy of Central Europe, with exiled princes, ruthless usurpers, beautiful damsels in distress, faithful and dishonest officials, all in an exaggerated and grotesque style that accentuates the woodenness of the characters and where the unreality of Mandrake jibes with the fatuity of the whole. That is, to solve the problem of Mandrake's credibility with a sort of homeopathic treatment, fakery against fakery.

Third solution: the Child. So let us try changing point of view, putting on a different pair of glasses, looking at Mandrake as his direct beneficiaries—that is, children—would see him. This allows us to take our distance from Mandrake and to be able to depict him with fond indulgence, with nostalgia-laden irony.

Let us imagine a child who is in bed with one of the many childhood maladies. When the worst has passed, the child asks his mommy to bring him his collection of Mandrake comics, his favorites. But mommy has taken advantage of the child's illness to "tidy up" his room and has thrown away everything she thought was outgrown, clutter, useless, including the Mandrake comics.

The child falls into despair. He cries. Night falls. Alone in his bed, he thinks of Mandrake. And lo and behold! Mandrake himself appears, preceded and heralded by the giant Lothar. "Did you think I had abandoned you?" smiles the Magician. "No, I'll never leave you. Come, let's go on a little trip together."

Thus, the child follows Mandrake in his adventures, at times participating in them, at times just watching or commenting or suggesting to Mandrake strategies that the latter had forgotten. The stories intertwine and, given the premises, can range from one genre to another, from one setting to another; a sort of "Opera Omnia" by Mandrake, reduced to short, incisive scenes. At the end of the film, Mandrake disappears and the child turns to other, more mature reading.

Fourth solution: the Orient. Mandrake studied magic in Tibet. His eternal rival is the Cobra, an oriental magician who has equally great powers, but turned to evil. Many adventures are set in India, or other unspecified places in Asia, where fakirs, priests, and initiates abound. This esoteric, magic, and religious aspect is very up-to-date today, with so many young people who escape to India or Nepal in search of a new spirituality, even through the agonizing experience of drugs.

Now, we are not saying that we ought to tell about an Asiatic Mandrake with an eye to young people and their religious aspirations, but it is in any case a fact that the magic world of the Far East now attracts a great deal of interest and that therefore our film would exploit subjects that are continuously examined by books and the mass media. Tibetan monasteries, opportunities to develop extraordinary, paranormal abilities in oneself, and so forth: themes and settings dear to Mandrake, that can be told in a slightly "high," dazzling, strange style.

Dimension X

Among these solutions, however, we have chosen a fifth. It is precisely the one suggested by the story entitled "Dimension X" (of 1937).

Here, there is the fascination of science fiction still at its beginnings, and we can work with nostalgia, while still respecting, however, all the ideas, styles, and possibilities of a real story of adventure and fantasy.

The naive science fiction of the time, still echoing with the memory of Jules Verne and

H.G. Wells: a galactic and futuristic world, seen with the wide-open and enraptured eyes of the dreaming child. Crystal men, living houses, infernal contraptions, traps of all kinds, time machines, and in the middle of all this, Mandrake in tails with his cloak fluttering about him, as if he himself were the magician who brings to life all these sideshow marvels: the pastiche could be amusing, ironic, and have a sure hold on the public, since it merges the retro fashion with the current one of stellar travel.

What is the story of this "Dimension X"? Here it is, in brief (the original comic strip, of course, has been modified, mutilated, and enriched). A slightly mad scientist, with a pointed beard and bow tie, has built a Marvelous Machine with which, by means of molecular disintegration, people can be projected from our third dimension to a Dimension X: that is, to a very faraway, absurd, and mysterious world. And naturally, as always happens with these new inventions, a problem immediately arises: Princess Narda, who, as chance would have it, is the niece of the scientist, wanted to "test" the machine, and has disappeared in Dimension X, from which she has never returned.

Faced with this news, what could Mandrake do but leap headlong into the machine and have himself projected into Dimension X, in search of his beloved? And Lothar is right by his side, in fez and leopard skin: he does not really understand what it is all about, but he will always follow his master.

So we have Mandrake and Lothar setting out for a strange, unknown world, illuminated by a star-shaped crystal sun, like those lamps that can be seen in the entrance foyers of old palaces. Once there, they are immediately taken prisoner by metallic men who run on a wheel that is part of them, like motorscooters with a life of their own; entrapped in fine metal webs, our two friends are led off to work

88

in the coal mines (an essential food for our Motorscooter men), where they have the fortune to find Narda, she, too, demeaned by the work as coal miner.

Mandrake decides that he had better act with a little magic to get out of that situation, and, in fact, manages to free himself and the others, just when the men-motorscooters are attacked by their ancient enemy: the Firebird! It is a gigantic bird, completely in flames, that melts any metal it even comes close to. Taking advantage of the confusion, Mandrake & Co. flee, but they fall from the frying pan into the fire: that is, into the power of colossal carnivorous plants; and one of these grabs Narda, giving grounds for the direst of expections ....

The adventures come one right after another at the rapid pace of the flat, synthetic images of comic strips: almost like a fast succession of photographs; a series of figures in movement that have the enchantment of the films of Méliès, but current-day remakes, in splendid living color and spatial dimensions.

Now Mandrake and his friends, having penetrated deeply into an incredible savana (hands reach up from the swamp grabbing at them), meet up with the tribe of men who eat mud; Lothar is offered a nice, damp clod, but he hesitates. He has never liked mud very much. Mandrake steps in and voilà! the clod is transformed into a tasty roast chicken.

All this is followed through a telescope by the king of the crystal men. They need human skin to polish themselves and maintain their transparency, just as we use chamois cloths to clean our windshields. Hence, they are anxious to capture Mandrake and his troupe, to skin them and use their hides as chamois cloths.

Thus, our heroes are in a nasty spot. Captured by the crystal men, who fly in crystal airplanes in a completely transparent, sparkling world, Mandrake, Narda, and Lothar find themselves chained to crystal poles in an immense crystal kingdom. The king decides their fate: they will be killed and flayed. But Mandrake cannot allow this. Materializing from nothing a pile of rocks, he can stone his enemies who shatter like Bohemian glasses. They manage to escape. But they are followed. The enemies are many, an army of crystal soldiers. They make a breathless escape; they fall into a lake inhabited by dreadful monsters; they manage to escape once again thanks to Mandrake's skills ... they finally reach the Mudeaters and the Motorscooter men, implacable enemies of the Crystal King.

Now comes the decisive battle: but how will they defeat that crystal army, so efficient, compact, jagged, hard, cold, inhumane (almost a foreshadowing of Nazism)?

Mandrake has colossal slingshots constructed, from which are launched fiery missiles: the smoke they produce will make the crystal men and their houses black and sooty, so our heroes will take the victory .... And they do not lose time in running to their Marvelous Machine, to return finally to the old world of the Third Dimension, but alas! A sad surprise! The Cobra, Mandrake's eternal enemy, has put the machine out of order.

How did the Cobra get to Dimension X? Thanks to the exceptional powers that his Tibetan origins have given him. In fact, the Cobra got to Dimension X traveling on an Indian monastery which acted as his spaceship: and now we see the monastery up there, suspended in the sky, hovering majestically among the clouds.

But who is that at one of the monastery's windows, waving her arms and crying for help? Princess Narda! But how could that be, if just a few minutes ago she was together with Mandrake and Lothar? Just a minute of distraction was enough for the Cobra to kidnap her, just like a suitcase swiped at the train station.

This launches a new series of adventures which will see the headlong clash of two irreducible enemies: Cobra and Mandrake. First off, in order to reach the hovering monastery, Mandrake begins to grow, he becomes gigantic, immense; he touches the monastery with his head, and Lothar swiftly climbs up his master's body as if he were scaling a mountain. Then Mandrake returns to his normal appearance and sets off in search of Narda, the eternal kidnapping victim.

This monastery, thanks to the skillful perfidy of the Cobra, is a small world, where the space could suddenly open out into a garden, or overlook small mountains and similar such fake landscapes that conceal traps, tricks, evil lures. There is even a giant bowling alley with colossal pins and balls the size of hot-air balloons that roll threateningly, trying to crush Mandrake and Lothar.

There is a gorilla with a human brain who keeps sharp watch and struggles with Lothar (the beast is killed). There are the mummies of old monks who rise from their tombs and march compactly against the invaders, but Mandrake, with a wave of his hand, surrounds them with fire and they turn to ash. Then there is the direct battle with the Cobra in person: the two great magicians struggle blow for blow with miracles and wonders of all kinds, transforming themselves, vanishing, taking one another by surprise, in a series of lightninglike gags, almost like cartoons. Finally, we learn that Narda has been captured by Zera, a terrible woman as white as snow, who turns everything she touches to ice. Zera also manages to trap Lothar and Mandrake in two large ice spheres, like soap bubbles. But here again, Mandrake escapes with his magic: he moves the sun so that it filters in through the window, striking Zera in full, who melts just like snow in the sun.

Down in the dungeons are all Zera's victims, motionless in ice coffins. Narda, too, is there, her eyes wide open. Mandrake quickly revives her, and now it is time to start thinking seriously about the return ... the Marvelous Machine is soon repaired ... and our troupe returns from Dimension X back to the Third Dimension ... Narda is reunited with her uncle and family ... but the adventures may continue.

Since, enclosed within the framework we have presented, the events and the episodes may be interchanged, substituted, stretched out, shortened, this has just been an example, to give an idea of the plot.

And what is most important in this plot is the archaic and infantile world of a form of science fiction where the fiction counted more than the science. A play-world, of machines and gadgets constructed like the toys of the time: tin, wood, string, springs. Only in this ironic dimension of a Méliès- or Verne-style vision is it possible to lead Mandrake into the atmosphere that most suits him: that of a whopping practical joke, of a spectacular fraud, of a breathtaking, rapid-fire series of tricks, like the ultra-fast cars of the flying eight.

"Lettere simpatiche" (Nice Letters) was what Fellini wrote on the file containing those that had given him the greatest pleasure, had aroused his curiosity, or had amused him.

Glancing through the director's vast unpublished correspondence (this is kept in his archives or in the Cinema Archives at the Center for the Arts, Art Department, Wesleyan University, Middletown, Connecticut), one is struck by fact that the majority of his official correspondents wrote to ask him for something. In particular, they wanted Fellini to accept prizes and go to receive them; be present at retrospectives, conferences, ceremonies, and seminars devoted to him; take part in commemorations, congresses, or film festivals; give his support to cultural, social, or political initiatives; write texts in honor of other great film-makers. These were all events that Fellini tried, as far as possible, to avoid—and he was usually successful. His replies were nearly always negative, politely accompanied by excuses, lies, and inventions, which were all intended to make the recipients forgive his unwillingness to take part.

The "Lettere simpatiche" are quite a different matter: they are expressions of friendship, correspondence regarding his work, and exchanges of information with film-maker and writer friends; missives showing interest, admiration, and solidarity. In his letters, Fellini used a style that was colloquial, straightforward, and light-hearted, even when he was addressing the president of the French Republic.

The unpublished letters written by, or to, Fellini, presented here in chronological order, all involve famous correspondents. All except one, that is: this is reproduced here as an example of the epistolary extravagance to which a great film director can be subjected.

Rome, April 26, 1974

Dear Ms. Cavani,

When I heard about the confiscation of your film *Il portiere di notte* (*The Night Porter*), my first reaction was the somewhat gloomy inertia with which one resigns oneself to serious, but normal, events, and to their habitual ineluctability. I do not wish to disappoint you with this cynicism, which not even the bitterness, the sense of mortification from which it derives, authorizes and justifies. I am well aware that this impassive dismay is perhaps the most alarming consequence of the vast, obscure operation that has been underway for some time now in this country, having as its objective the elimination of every endeavor and every commitment embodying the vital, free processes of culture.

What can be done about this? How many protests, motions, manifestos, petitions, and telegrams have I signed in the last few years? But all to no avail! How can we change the indolent, conservative, childish mentality of us Italians, which always tends to identify itself with collective schemes and not take up individual positions? How can we extirpate the bewildering conditioning to which we have been subjected, when we do not even know whether it is the result of a precise design or if it is, rather, just a sort of perpetual motion that is both anonymous and mechanical. Sometimes I think, selfishly no doubt, that if we are not able to change this country, despite the good will of so many people, then it would be better to change country in the other sense, that is, to go to live elsewhere.

There is one thing that makes me really angry: that, in our democratic system, it is not possible to find a way of preventing abuses of power of this kind. However, I am willing to participate in any concrete initiatives that you may wish to take to protect our work. Naturally, I shall participate with my usual enthusiasm and mistrust.

With my warmest regards,
Federico Fellini

Frederico,

Je voulais t'écrire le jour même de notre rencontre, puis le lendemain, puis chaque jour... mais le programme d'un voyageur est imprévisible, le mien en tout cas est fort chargé, et ce n'est qu'aujourd'hui que je peux enfin réaliser mon souhait.

Bien sur, je tenais à exprimer les remerciements comme il est d'usage... mais la force de ce que j'ai vécu au cours de notre rencontre est telle que le cadre des usages me semble éclater en mille morceaux.

Je sens encore la bonne énergie qui m'a soudain enveloppé dès que nous nous sommes vus, comme si un ange nous entourait de son aura chaleureuse.

Je sens encore la bonté de tes bras lorsque tu m'as étreint contre toi, comme si j'étais soudain un jeune garçon serré affectueusement par un oncle gigantesque...

Quelle expérience, j'avais rarement été plongé dans un tel bain de jubilation intérieure, avec une si belle mousse de satisfaction intellectuelle et un tel parfum de justesse spirituelle.

Je vais arrêter de violer ta modestie avec mes compliments, on a déjà dû te les faire mille fois, sache cependant que tu as fait un très beau cadeau à Moebius et que l'oeil qui aide à choisir les bonnes lumières n'a pas été reçu sur le plan uniquement matériel.

J'espère avoir encore l'occasion de te retrouver... en attendant je te souhaite bonne vie, avec amour, amours et lumières, et lumière!!!

Jean "Moebius" Giraud

POUR FREDERICO

Federico,

I wanted to write to you on the very day that we met, then the day after, then every day.... But the program of a traveler is unpredictable, and mine, in any case is very full. It is only today that I have managed to send you my best wishes.

Naturally I wanted to express my gratitude, as one normally does.... But the impact of what I experienced during our meeting is such that "normality" seems to me to have exploded into a thousand pieces.

I can still feel the energy that suddenly enveloped me when we met, as if an angel had surrounded me with its warm aura.

I can still feel the goodness of your arms when you embraced me, as if I had suddenly become a small boy who was being affectionately hugged by a gigantic uncle....

What an experience! Rarely have I been immersed in a such a bath of inner joy, with such a wonderful foam of intellectual satisfaction and such a perfume of spiritual perfection.

Now I will stop offending your modesty with my compliments; although you must be very used to this, you should be aware that you have done Moebius a world of good, and that the eye that helps one to find good lights has been received not only on a material plane.

I hope I shall have the opportunity to meet you again.... While awaiting this event, I wish you a happy life, with love, loves and lights, and light!

Jean "Moebius" Giraud

Bologna, March 12, 1979

Dear Mr. Fellini,

The day before yesterday I saw *Prova d'or-chestra* (*Orchestra Rehearsal*), and yesterday I saw it again. It really is extraordinarily rich in detail; on seeing it again, I continually discovered things that I had missed the first time.

I see that it is a film which, unfortunately, is open to misunderstanding. Possibly this is because it expresses an idea that is, in my opinion, very precious, and as indispensable as that of the social order that enables human beings to live together; it is a concept of profound antisociality, in which one's neighbor is, at the same time, viewed with passion and repugnance. Each individual has unique qualities, but the result is often, I am sorry to say, forced cohabitation: I believe that this contradiction is the leaven of the film.

Perhaps you are not aware of the extent to which the lives of very many people (like myself, for example) would be different without your films.

Thanks a lot.
Yours,

Carlo Ginzburg

Paris

Just seen *Prova* what a masterpiece congratulations regards

Peter Brook

Fårö, July 11, 1979

Dear Federico,

It was so good to hear from you after all these years, but you are never far away. A few days ago I saw your *Amarcord* for the seventh time, I think it is one of the most wonderful pictures ever made.

As you perhaps know, I live in Munich since 1976 and if your friend wants to see me he can call me, Telephone 89/981554 or write me a letter address Titurelstrasse 2, 8000 München 81, after September 18.

I wish you all the best for your work. When you talk about hard labor, I must confess, I feel exactly the same, every morning when I have to go to the studio.

Dear brother and friend I'm looking forward to seeing you sometime, somewhere.

Ingmar Bergman

New York, November 18, 1980

Dear Mr. Fellini,

It was fine to hear from you again. I very well remember the night at Jackie's, and how much I wanted to talk to you, and how much everybody else did, too. But we did meet once again at some party that was given for the opening of one of your pictures, although I cannot remember which one, and I did try once again to express my admiration for you and your work, but there were too many young beauties around you to allow me the time or the space.

Anyway, here it is now, my admiration, I mean, and my pleasure that Hammett's work interests you. Among the Hammett material you want, this is the story: "The Tenth Clue" is owned by me and is thus available to you. "The Golden Horseshoe". This was bought by Grimaldi but my guess is that it could be bought back from him, and either I could try to do that, or depending on your relationship with Grimaldi, it might be better if you tried. I have only met him once, and the negotiations for all the Hammett stuff he bought were done through my agent.

"The House in Turk Street" is owned by me and is thus available to you.

"The Girl with Silver Eyes" was also bought by Grimaldi.

"The Whosis Kid" is owned by me and is thus available to you.

"The Main Death" is owned by me and is thus available to you.

There are a number of Hammett stories which have not been bought by anybody. Some of them I like very much, but I don't see them as fitting in with his other stories. Some of them I don't like at all and kept them from being published because I thought they were not good enough. I would not allow many people to see them, but I would Xerox them for you if you feel that, after an effort, the Grimaldi negotiations cannot be made. In the meantime I wanted to hurry this letter off to you, and I send you my friendliest greetings and, through the years, my great admiration.

Lillian Hellman

(*to Maggie and Ray Bradbury*)
Rome, December 28, 1980

Dear Maggie and dear Ray,

Your greetings noted with the lovely poem (which I had translated by the splendid girl who is now translating this letter) pleased me immensely.

What a pity that you don't live in Rome, or at least in a town a bit closer than Los Angeles, because you really inspire the idea that you are the ideal friends, those with whom one is well even in silence.

Dear Ray, of course I'd like to make a movie with you, and I would do it right away! But you see how lazy I am, how unwilling and how I give up before starting, and precociously aged, imagine that at only sixtyone, I already look over forty. How often I've been offered to made a movie in America, and I kept on saying no, pulling out heaps of excuses which sounded even convincing, justified, actually, when I recite them, I see that I put on a good show for myself, and I am looked upon with esteem, I am approved of with great participation about the artist's reasons, this artist who can only express himself in his own language, who cannot deroot himself, etc. etc....

The truth is I should try dropping everything and try to be reborn somewhere else. Who knows if I'll manage to be convinced sooner or later? I'd have plenty of motives, the way things are going over here, it couldn't be worse, and the image of the immigrant is fully justified.

I don't know. In the meanwhile I'm preparing another movie. Will I really start it? It's become so difficult to get a picture standing, and when you do, you even feel slightly embarassed to actually make it, because in this life which is so drammatical and desperate, making a movie seems a very frivolous thing to do. On the other hand, it's the only thing I know how to do. I should start shooting in March. I'd like to tell you the story, and have your opinion, but the splendid girl is fretting, it's getting dark, it's snowing outside and she has to go to a party somewhere. I must end here.

I embrace you, dear Ray, with brotherly affection, and I truly hope to see you soon. Best wishes to Maggie as well.

With my warmest wishes for your work, good luck,

Federico

December 22, 1981

Dear Federico:

    First let me say how wonderful it was to meet you. Rarely has anyone I've admired so much turned out to be such a warm person. Deborah and I both enjoyed lunch thoroughly and look forward to our next meeting.
I went to see "AN AMERICAN WEREWOLF IN LONDON" at the Rivoli Saturday night and was appalled by the dreadful mix done in Rome at the time of dubbing the film into Italian. I was also dismayed by the quality of the print, and imagine my surprise when there suddenly appeared an intermission! Oh well. I should learn by now that I will always be disappointed when seeing my films in a commercial cinema.

    I hope you do consider coming on to Los Angeles when you next visit New York. My invitation to stay at our house is very sincere, and if you'd rather stay in a hotel, I know I can show you a Los Angeles that others would not.

    I am forever grateful to Mario for introducing us. Please give my best to your assistant.

    Deborah joins me in sending you and your family our very best wishes for a merry christmas and a joyous and prosperous new year. Much love.

John Landis

First draft of correspondence between Fellini and Elia [Kazan?].

Rome, May 31, 1983

Dear Mr. Kubrick,

Forgive me for distracting you from your work with a request for advice, but I don't know who to turn to. It's about this: I have to dub my latest picture (*E la nave va*) into English. The film has been shot for the most part in English with British actors, but I really can't take the responsibility of taking care of the final version in a language which I know only very approximately.

Could you maybe indicate me someone who could take charge of following the dubbing of my film, choosing the writer for the translation, adapting the "lipsing" for the Italian lines, choosing voices and directing the actors? That is to say, someone that disposing of time and means could do this work in a decent way? The dubbing would be done in London, and most of the actors, being British, could dub themselves. Once again forgive me for this little bother I am giving you, but I turn to you with great trust because I know how much you love this work and the perfection with which you realize it. I wish you all the best with your work, and send you my best greetings with affection and admiration.

Sincerely,
Federico Fellini

excerpt, c. 1983

Even though they are "work" photos, I would certainly prefer two stills of *Casanova*. They are all magnificent. One or two from *Roma* (e.g., the cardinals' fashion parade) and two or three from *E la nave va*, which I must have seen nine or ten times. I'll return the photos; please send them to me!

A big hug and thank you for existing!
Your Leonor Fini

February 21, 1984

Dear Federico,

Naturally, being a Greek, I am a partisan of Greek directors. You've probably seen the work of Theo Angelopoulos. The other Greek director, not as well known outside of Greece as yet, but equally able, equally honest and strong, is Pantelis Voulgaris.

He has written a scenario which I have read and asked me to recommend him to R.A.I., to Dottore Canepari, which I have done. Here is a man who deserves all support and I want to give him all of mine. So I am recommending him to you. He says that at a nod from the Dottore, he will come to Rome and I have suggested that he look you up. You will find a brother-artist there. And I will appreciate any and all help you can give him.

He has some money from the Greek government for the film he proposes making. But naturally this is a small amount. He hopes to influence R.A.I. for more financial help. You must know that I wouldn't presume on our friendship unless I was abundantly convinced of this man's importance and worth.

My warmest regards
Elia Kazan

Beverly Hills, California, August 29, 1986

Dear Federico,

I'm coming to Rome for four days on Saturday, September 13 through Wednesday, September 17. I'll be at the De La Ville. I hope to see you.

I'm now 6 feet, 2 inches tall with a tremendous amount of black hair and a perfect body. What do you look like?

Best wishes,
Paul Mazursky

May 5, 1987

Dear Mr. Fellini,

An old lady does not only think about her past, but she must also concern herself about what will happen after her death.
In short, I am a very wealthy woman, and I do not have any heirs!

For years I have taken an interest in your work; I deeply admire your creative activity, and I would be very happy to know that my fortune was in your hands after my death.
I would, therefore, be delighted if you would agree to become my heir: this would also permit me to express the admiration that I feel for the Italians, whom I have come to know in the numerous, unforgettable visits I have made to your country with my deceased husband.

As soon as you inform me that you accept my proposal, I will draw up my last will and testament. I am certain that this financial support will help you to continue your extremely important work.

Yours sincerely,
Carola v. Gästern

Note: This interesting letter, which was followed by further correspondence, turned out to be a hoax by a German writer. However, as may be seen from one of his replies, it was a trap into which Fellini did not fall.

Rome, June 25, 1987

Dear Madame,

When, at last, I received your letter, this dispelled my suspicion that the whole affair could be nothing more than a hoax organized, perhaps, by pranksters on the staff of a magazine in search of an idea for the summer. But your second letter has reassured me!

A haunted castle? But this is my ideal castle, just what I have always wanted!

So, what happens next, my dear Madame Gerda? I am waiting to receive the keys in my robust hands. Meanwhile, I wish to thank you: I believe you have had a truly wonderful idea.

I have noted a small mistake in your first letter, in which there was a stamp representing the castle of Fillerschloss. Here it was written "350 Jahre," while you told me that it dated back to the fourteenth century, adding, therefore, 200 years. What should I tell my expert friends?

I send you my best regards,

Federico Fellini

P.S. Another question: in view of the donation, have you been obliged to change both your given name and surname?

Lausanne, January 19, 1988

Dear Federico,

I am always amazed when I hear what you are doing, whether directly from you or from the newspapers. I believe that you are an exception, not only on account of your extraordinary talent, but also because you are one of the rare people, if not the only one, who is able to create in the midst of perpetual chaos, with precision and assurance that cannot fail to astound those like myself, who can only work in calm, quiet surroundings, in complete reclusion, even. And, on each occasion, you manage to surprise us, and this bears witness to your wealth of ideas that nothing around you can disturb.

Your new film is a further evidence of this. I cannot wait to talk to you about it. In fact, dear Fellini, you remind me of a permanent firework display pouring out stars of many colors, one more brilliant than the other.

I send a big hug to you; please hug Giulietta for me and share my affection with her.

Your old friend,

Georges Simenon

P.S. Yesterday evening, on the Swiss television, I watched *Ginger and Fred*. It was a real joy to see it. Giulietta was really outstanding: she was all the Giuliettas in one!

(*to Giorgio La Malfa, secretary of the Partito Repubblicano Italiano-PRI*)

Rome, May 9, 1989

Dear Mr. La Malfa,

First of all I would like to say how sorry I am that I have not been able to speak to you directly. I know that your secretary has unsuccessfully tried to get in touch with me a number of times, but the film I am making at present has kept me very busy over the last few weeks, away from the studios and, therefore, difficult to contact. Please accept my apologies.

I would have liked to thank you in person for the invitation that you sent to me through our friend Biasini; this has touched me deeply. At the same time, I would like to express my sincere gratitude for the measures that your party has taken to eliminate, or, at least, to mitigate, the particularisms and conflicts that appear to dominate the political and social life of our country today.

Moreover, the high esteem and deep affection that I always felt for your father—the memory of his profound humanity, perspicacity, and integrity are still vivid in my mind—have strengthened my desire to encourage you to persevere with the project that is so dear to your heart.

On the other hand, I cannot but confirm that my tendency—my instinctive predisposition—to avoid participating actively in politics is counterbalanced by my total involvement in my work. This leaves little time for commitments that, because of their seriousness, would absorb a considerable amount of time and energy.

I regret, therefore, that, after careful consideration, I feel that I must decline your invitation, tempting though it may be. I would like to thank you once again and send you my warmest regards.

I would very much like to meet you, dear Mr. La Malfa, and, should you have a free moment, I would be very honored if you could pay us a visit at the studios where I am working at present. Would this be possible? Wishing you all the best with your work, and good luck,

Yours,
Federico Fellini

(to François Mitterand, President of the Republic of France)

Rome, December 5, 1989

Dear Mr. Mitterand,

I would like to compliment you on the marvelous festival that you have offered us film-makers, devotees of the cinema, and the general public. In general, these occasions are characterized by a sense of detachment and boredom, since they are rituals that are repeated year after year, becoming merely a source of irritation, so that in the end, despite the fact that they are intended to help the cinema, they make it seem duller and more outmoded than before.

I have been fortunate enough to enjoy every moment of this exciting, joyful festival. Congratulations, Mr. Mitterand. Everything went very smoothly and the inevitable hitches were resolved with good humor, because they really seemed to have been deliberately planned! Everything was to my liking: the evocation of the *Potemkin*, and the fact that we were able to find, all together like schoolchildren, the old actors of the French theater and cinema, was both deeply moving and very entertaining.

I prefer not to speak about my own role, because it makes me feel even more guilty about not having been there in person to thank you for the affection that you have shown me.

Congratulations, Mr. Mitterand. May I also compliment you on your stage presence: the charming and authoritative manner in which you presented this cinema festival will be remembered as a splendid example for others to follow.

I thank you from the bottom of my heart and hope to have the pleasure of meeting you in the near future in order to be able to express in person the high esteem in which I hold you. May I wish you all the best with your work and good luck.

Federico Fellini

(Response by Fellini to Kurosawa's Publicity Manager for comments about Rhapsody in August, *released in 1991)*

After I had seen this film by Akira Kurosawa, I felt as if I had returned to my home town, that time had stood still and death had been dissipated. I was sitting in my grandmother's kitchen, listening to her tales, basking in the warmth of her affection, and drinking in her astounding knowledge of life.

It is true that *Rhapsody in August* stoically addresses the theme of the atomic bomb, one of the great tragedies of this century. But the most outstanding feature of the film is, in my opinion, the way it manages, in the simple, everyday manner of a children's story, to deal with questions regarding our deepest feelings, family bonds, and the mysteries that shroud our existence.

Nowadays Kurosawa speaks with the freedom of the prophet, ignoring all the rules, above the tricks and the compromises of our trade. Apart from being a marvelous film-maker, he is a great sage who marches ahead of us, showing us the path to take.

Federico Fellini

Anthony Quinn
60 East End Avenue
New York, New York 10028

September 17, 1990

Caro Federico e Giulietta,

    Vi ringrazio tanto per quello che avete
detto di me sull'intervista che trattava della
mia carriera.

    Per me, tutti e' due rimanete il punto
piu' alto della mia vita.

    Ho imparato tanto di voi.

    Parlo sempre del 'Strange man', called
Fellini -- and the 'sweet lost girl, Gelsomina',
che e' Giulietta.

    Sono molto grato e lo saro' sempre.

    Con amore a tutti e' due.

Antonio
Q

Rome Address: Vigna San Antonio
Cecchina di Roma - Italy

September 17, 1990

Dear Federico and Giulietta,

    I wish to thank you very much for what you said about me in the interview regarding my career.

    For me, you are both the high point of my life.

    I have learnt a lot from you both.

    I often speak about the "Strange man" called Fellini—and the "sweet lost girl, Gelsomina," in other words, Giulietta.

    I am very grateful, and I shall always be so. With love to you both.

Antonio
Q

September 10, 1993

Dear Mr. Fellini,

    As you read this, I hope you are feeling a lot better, I have been a fan of yours ever since I could see, and was deeply touched when through Gerry Lewis I learned of your congratulations to me for the Golden Lion. It is an additional thrill to know I've been awarded the same honor you received for your body of your work, recognized and saluted a few years back.

    Your films have been a great source of inspiration for me. They have contributed more than most other movies in defining film as art. I'm sorry I didn't get a chance to see you in Venice, but I'm sure our paths will cross in the future. All my best, as I continue to look at your films and gain more and more inspiration.

Your friend,
Steven Spielberg

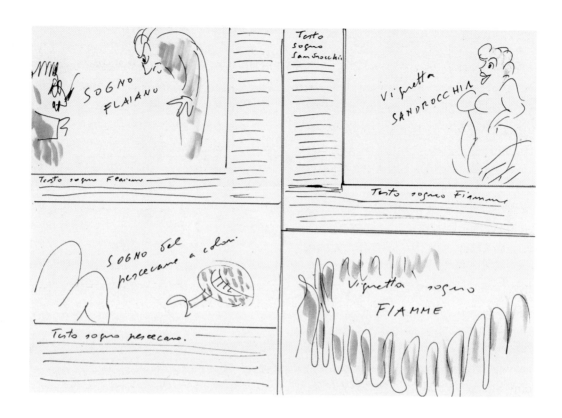

The Book of Dreams

In 1960 Federico Fellini began to log what he remembered of his dreams by means of sketches and writings. It all started when he decided to explain one of his dreams to the renowned Jungian analyst [Ernest] Bernhard by sketching it out on paper; Bernhard suggested that Fellini keep a systematic record of his dreams—particularly those that were less immediately comprehensible. For over twenty years, therefore, Fellini compiled these records of his dreams. The books themselves, the "Libri dei sogni" (Books of Dreams), are weighty leather-bound volumes of white drawing paper, with drawings and writings in ink and felt-tip pen. One of these books has been lost: Fellini lent it to a group of American psychoanalysts, who never returned it. Another volume disappeared when the Fellinis moved.

Fellini was a great dreamer, even as a child. "When I was about six or seven," he wrote, "I was convinced that we lived two existences—one with our eyes open, and one with them closed. I couldn't wait to go to bed in the evening. I'd named the four posts of my bed after the four movie theaters in Rimini—Fulgor, Savoia, Opera Nazionale Balilla, and Sultano. The show began the moment I closed my eyes. First a velvety darkness, deep and transparent, a darkness that led into another kind of darkness. Then the darkness was punctuated by flashes: a bit like the sea at night, when a storm is brewing and the horizon is bombarded by lightning. Then I would slip in even deeper, and the flashes showered all around me. Colored spirals appeared, rays of light, constellations, luminous points, gleaming spheres sometimes crowned with rings like the planet Saturn. The dark sky was punctuated with dazzling points of glowing color, which gradually began to rotate, with me as the hub. This spectacle had me spellbound. As it revolved, the splendor of this galaxy of light dwindled bit by bit and slowed down, rather like a playground ride losing its momentum. Everything was becoming more torpid, more pale. This meant that the show in that corner had come to an end, and so I switched to the next bedpost. Once again the swirling colors appeared, and light spread everywhere, and then went out again. And on to the next bedpost—the show went on all through the night. For years. They were not real dreams as such: I could still hear the voices and sounds from the house...."

Toward the end of his life Fellini dreamed a lot less, or he was less able to recollect them. "Seeing as I suffer from insomnia," he explained, "I have to take tranquillizers and sedatives, and these all tend to impair one's ability to dream, they kill mental images. I must say that, despite these pills and tablets, and despite my being rather less effervescent than I was at thirty or forty, at the end or beginning of each new film I have a dream that ties in with what I'm doing, a dream that in some subtle way offers a foretaste of the result and the way the film will be received."

Notwithstanding the persistence of many international publishers, the drawings and texts of Fellini's "Libri dei Sogni" have never been compiled and made public. Excerpts have appeared in the monthly journal *Dolce vita* (1987, no. 3; 1988, no. 12), edited by Lietta Tornabuoni, and in another monthly *Il Grifo* (1991, nos. 1–9), edited by Vincenzo Mollica; some of those excerpts reappear here.

As everyone knows, dreams are mysterious things. Any account of a dream is what the dreamer manages to recall upon waking: and in the process of relating, writing down, or sketching ideas from a dream, the dreamer inevitably filters and adjusts it to waking life, expressing it in his or her aesthetic style. In fact, Fellini later made stylistic adjustments to some of these dream accounts, including corrections and crossings out.

The following pages contain reproductions of some of the annotated drawings Fellini made to describe his dreams. A printed transcription of the text is provided below, and in many cases there is a note with additional background information or clues to the content of the dream. Where available we have also reported the dreamer's comments or off-the-cuff interpretations (often mocking or sidetracking) given in the course of interviews.

The Cardinal. Text of a dream of April 15, 1961:

"In a dark room weakly illuminated by candles, Cardinal Montini stares into the darkness with his icy eyes. I decide to confront him.

'Your Eminence, do you trust me?' I ask.

'Not at all,' he replies acidly. It is evident that he does not believe for a moment the Christian message that critics, scholars, and priests have found in my films.

'Do you think I am religious?' I ask again.

'Oh, yes I do!' he replies at once. 'One can see from your face that you're religious.'

'What splendid eyes you have, Cardinal!' I say rather obsequiously...."

Note: The Milanese Jesuits of San Fedele had defended *La dolce vita* in one of their journals. The archbishop of Milan at that time, Monsignor Montini, who later became Pope Paul VI, severely punished this expression of approval. Feeling that he was, at least in part, responsible, Fellini asked for an audience with Monsignor Montini. Fellini recounted: 'Montini did not say a single word, he listened to me without looking at me. Finally, he said, 'I will pray to the Lord in order that he may enlighten you.' And that was all."

Going Backward. Text of a dream of June 23, 1974:

"It is a terrible night. *I* am driving a black automobile that is going backward at breakneck speed along a track that winds around a mountain. I am not able to slow down, although I am pressing the brake pedal with all my might. On my right there is a precipice. The drivers of the cars coming in the opposite direction flash their lights in terror...."

Note: Fellini considered this dream to be an obvious manifestation of fear and self-imprisonment, recommending that we not attribute ethical, ideological, or aesthetic meanings to the backward motion of the car. The director had stopped driving in 1970.

Question Marks. Text of a dream of August 22, 1974:

'Oreste del Buono (the journalist and writer) is watching me. I indicate to him that I am busy, and, somewhat unwillingly, I show him the work I am engaged in: this consists of describing large question marks on a sheet of paper with a brush loaded with red paint. Del Buono watches in silence with a friendly air, but it seems to me that his eyes are smiling ironically. And the question marks change, perhaps because the paintbrush is too wet, they fade, they almost disappear.... N.B. Del Buono has always shown enthusiasm for the film about Casanova.'

Note: In the same period other dreams reflect the state of mind of Fellini, whose patience had been sorely tried by the long wait to begin work on *Casanova*: the producers De Laurentiis and Rizzoli had withdrawn from the project, which was then suspended until 1975, when the producer Grimaldi stepped in.

Acoustic Glue. Text of a dream of October 30, 1974:
'Someone had called me on the phone and was speaking to me in a very confused manner. The intonation of his voice gave what he said a sense of familiarity, and he always seemed to be about to understand, but, on the whole, there was a sort of acoustic glue, something echoing that made the words and the overall sense of the what he was saying absolutely incomprehensible....'

On the Tracks. Text of a dream of October 30, 1974:

"Who are you talking to? Who's that?' I only remember the scene as I have attempted to draw it. No train could be seen on the horizon, nor could the noise of wheels that would herald it be heard; I did not even know if and when a train would go by. Despite this, thinking about it now that I am awake, the situation does not seem to be reassuring. What do you think?"

Note: This situation, which was repeated in other dreams, was used by Fellini, with some varia- tions, in one of the commercials he made for the Banca di Roma with Paolo Villaggio and Anna Franchi. The interpretation that the director gave to it referred to his private life: 'Let us suppose that a lady has up- braided me because I have been neglecting her, and she has insist- ed that we should have a little more time together.... Perhaps the dream is an attempt to warn me, with the metaphor of the meal on the rail- road track, that our relationship might be threatened by gossip. Perhaps the dream is courteously telling me to inform the lady, in a tactful way, possibly by phone."

Lucianona. Text of a dream of January 1, 1975:

'A hypnagogic image. As she appeared in the Christmas issue of *Vogue* some years ago, Lucianona invaded the blue space of a vast expanse of sky over the sea at Focene, in which there were long white-crested waves. She looked downward with eyes shining with joy, and, parting her immense fleshy pink lips she said to a brown shadow behind her (Lothar), 'They have surrendered! We have won even before the fight has begun!'

Together with the striking figure, there was a strong smell of the sea, just as there is in Rimini at the end of the winter, a salty smell that was borne by the wind.'

Note: Fellini often had hypnagogic visions, induced by the process of falling asleep. Luciana Marcellini (Lucianona) had appeared in an ironical film-comic strip, together with Marcello Mastroianni as Mandrake, in the special issue of the French edition of *Vogue* produced by Fellini for Christmas 1972.

110

An Happy, unhappy. Text of a dream of January 21, 1975.
'*Infelice... Un felice*!!! An [*sic*]... happy? Oh, how unhappy I am!!! How do you spell it? An happy? Oh no, 'an happy' means 'un felice,' (a happy person) not infelice (an unhappy one).... What then?
I can neither proceed, nor can I reverse, nor can I go back to where I have come from. Blocked! Immobile.'

Note: Fellini interpreted the dream as follows: 'The dream of a verbal game may be an invitation to bear in mind that if you do not know English—a foreign language—very well, then, since the language of the unconscious is foreign to you, how can you allow yourself to decide about the meaning of things and to find definitions and diagnoses that are based on premises immersed in ignorance?'

A Gigantic Newborn Baby. Text of a dream of April 1, 1975:
'A hypnagogic image. P., naked and pink, like a gigantic newborn baby, was sitting on an immobile cloud in the midst of a bright blue sky. I felt the moment had come to do something, and I began to blow at the cloud, saying, 'It's time to fertilize what lies beneath.' Driven by the puff of air, as powerful as that of a god, P.'s cloud began to sail slowly and calmly across the sky. With a solemn gesture, P. raised her fabulous great breasts in her hands, and shining rain fell in an orderly manner on the earth. Well, well!'

112

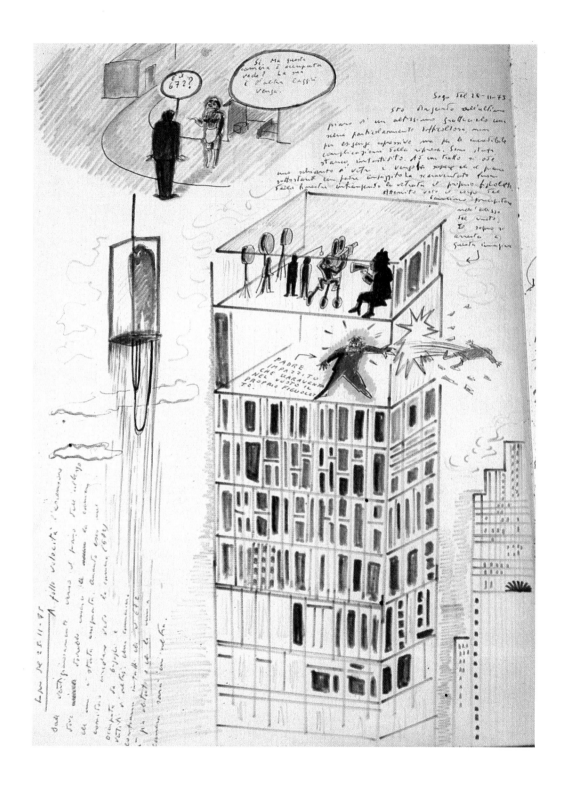

Breakneck Speed. Text of a dream of November 25, 1975:

'The elevator ascends at breakneck speed toward the floor of the hotel where the room that has been assigned to me ought to be. When I go out into the corridor, I see the room (672) is occupied by the baggage and clothes of other people. In fact, a maid confirms that room 672 is already occupied, and that my room must be another.'

Text of a dream of November 26, 1975:

'On the top floor of a very tall skyscraper, I am shooting a scene that is very difficult, not from the stylistic point of view, but rather because of incredible complica-tions in the shooting. I am very weary of the whole business. Suddenly, we hear the noise of break-ing glass, and I am informed that on the floor below a crazed father has hurled his own child out of the window, smashing the glass. Terri-fied, I watch the child's body fall into the abyss. At this point, the dream stops.'

Note: Fellini related this 'allegori-cal and dramatic tale of the un-conscious' to his state of mind— 'tormented, confused, impotent, and mortified'—which preceded the start of a number of films, es-pecially *8 1/2*; at a certain point he had attempted to abandon this film after months of doubts, anxie-ties, and sleepless nights.

Mastorna. Text of a dream of Sep-tember 9, 1978:

'The usual phenomenon of vibra-tion and vertical raising of my body toward the night sky. I am flying, and I am aware that I am ex-periencing the inexplicable, mys-terious adventure that began dur-ing the night when I was a child. I reach a great height in the dark-ness of the sky. I ask to see Mastorna, the man himself, his face, the elusive character who, for many years now, has obsessed me, following me and abandoning me. Suddenly, a large photograph appears, surrounded by a dark frame: it represents a man wearing a hat and holding a briefcase.
He has a black moustache and his velvety eyes are also black.

It is Mastorna!
The place where the photograph was taken seems to be the vast concourse of a railroad station.
At the very moment that I recog-nize my protagonist, the vibration ceases, I am no longer flying, and I have the physical sensation that I am waking up in an enormous, bare room.
Here the dream continues: stand-ing on my left, Giulietta prevents me from seeing the end of the bed (where the photograph of Mastorna appeared) by holding the top of the sheet or a napkin in front of my eyes. She does this two or three times; two little girls on my right seem to be amused by these goings-on and laugh guile-lessly.'

The Wild Beasts. Text of a dream of June 22, 1980.

"While crossing a dark forest at night, I come to a brightly illuminated clearing where the painter of wild beasts lives and works. I see him from behind: he is a robust sixty-year-old, with his gray hair cut short in military fashion. With his brushes, canvas, and palette, he is busy painting portraits of some lionesses that prowl, sinuously and powerfully, around him. Although their white eyes flash, they are happy to have their portraits painted. Some pose, smiling with mouths that have human lips, and their eyes have a languid, feminine expression, although they maintain a ferocious aspect. I try to move as little as possible: while I am not afraid, I am tense and careful. However, I feel protected by the presence of the painter, so that, with a torch that I find in my hands, I amuse myself by arousing the curiosity of a wild beast and bewildering it by shining the light onto the ground a few inches from its greedy, murderous face, and slowly moving the circle of light, which the animal follows, cautiously but hungrily sniffing at it...."

Note: In this dream, Fellini saw a reference to women and the preparations for *La città delle donne*: "It's a story of good omen. I am able to tackle the wild beasts that are inside me. The painter manages to overcome his fear and is able to depict the fascinating threat...."

Note: Although the following drawings are from Fellini's dream notebooks, they lack the date and the original text, in compliance with the wishes of the director, who preferred to explain them with the brief texts published here.

Giuseppe Verdi. 'Where is this airplane going? On its right wing, there are four young girls with big fat asses that make it fly all askew. The sky was red.... 'If we are stowaways, it is the captain's fault!' the four sang softly in chorus; they were stark naked, plump, and red in the glare of the sunlight. And, as they bounced on their magnificent buttocks, they laughed.

I may have woken up at this point, because I thought I could see the light of dawn through the curtains. 'But I want to sleep a little longer, I want to continue the dream of the airplane,' I said. And I tried hard to see the fiery red sky again. Instead, the face of an old man with white hair came toward me out of a dense blue shadow, as if he had been blown by the wind, and, under his bushy white eyebrows, his two light blue eyes stared at me limpidly and implacably. It was Giuseppe Verdi....'

Giovanni Agnelli. "I was a guest at Agnelli's home. There were a lot of people: fellow film-makers, actresses, assistants. There had been a splendid party with a dinner and dancing, and now, late at night, the most privileged of us were all together in Agnelli's huge bed; he was wearing very elegant pajamas of shiny silk, with sky-blue and white stripes.

I was lying near him and I could see his face very clearly: I thought he looked aged and weary. It took him a long time to turn his head to look at me. There was embarrassment in his eyes, and I thought I could detect deep dissatisfaction and the sting of remorse, which regarded both of us. Then the naked woman who had been lying between us sat up; she seemed to have been offended by our apathy. She got out of bed and, displaying her splendid round bottom, she went toward the garden that could be seen through the picture window in the first light of dawn. Two men in white coats, rough and muscular, had been vigorously massaging Agnelli for some time...."

My End. "I am surrounded on three sides by very high flames; my back is to the wall of a deserted house, doors and windows are shut so that I cannot escape. On the other side of the barrier of fire, a group of German soldiers are loading their machine guns in order to hasten my end."

VISIONE · IPNAGOGICA

118

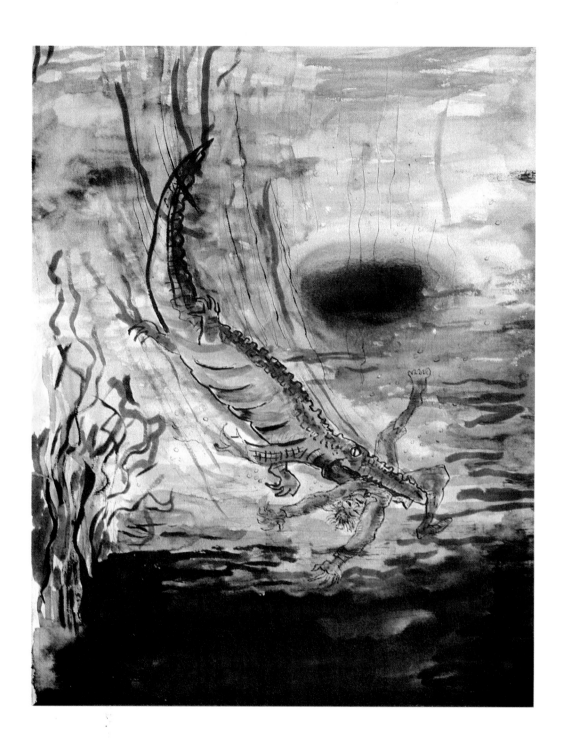

Ever darker. 'I did not know where I was; suddenly, an immense crocodile seized me by the waist and dragged me down endlessly into the ever darker abysses of the river....'

Sandrocchia. 'There is Sandrocchia (Sandra Milo) with her splendid smooth, warm belly, wrapped in a satin dress, with white fox furs on her voluptuous shoulders, just as she appeared in *Giulietta degli spiriti*.... I want to get rid of a small black and white monkey that continues to bite my left hand. It has not wounded me, and it does not even hurt me. On my skin, however, the imprint of its sharp little teeth has formed a sort of inscription. I look more closely and something really is written there: 'Be careful' it says. Later I found myself thinking, 'Be careful.' But who or what should I be careful of? And why is it written in English?'

The Female Warrior. "I seemed to have been expected in front of a cavern that suddenly opened in a rock face. Crouching down next to the dark entrance there is a powerful half-naked female figure with the ancient face of the peasant warrior.

'An Aztec?' I thought in the dream. There was something archaic in the mysterious inscription in the rock above the entrance to the cave. ('Everything that you can do has already been decided long ago!') The woman seemed to be looking at me through her half-closed eyes, perhaps without seeing me. She was both severe and conspiratorial, and a silence reigned that induced me to search in the depths of my memory. But what? And what was the meaning of that inscription? What was it? A verdict, a sentence? The revelation of the arcane? I was not able to move, I could not breathe, I was becoming a stone that was being smothered willy-nilly by the infinite gaze of the ancient priestess. Finally, a burst of laughter freed everything, and the carefree voice of a child squatting close by said exactly what I have written in the drawing. ('Yes! Yes! But you can always do a pooh!! Ah! Ah! Ah!') I woke up in a good mood, and I was not particularly concerned whether or not I understood my dream."

Film-Comic Strips

In the final years of his life—from the days of *La voce della luna* in 1989 to his death in 1993, Fellini no longer directed. When interviewed he tended somewhat nobly to hold himself responsible for this lack of output, putting it down to laziness, hesitancy, lack of motivation, lack of conviction. In fact, notwithstanding repeated contacts and negotiations, innumerable interviews and proposals, he was unable to find anyone to finance his projects, except for the television special *L'attore*: the economic crisis in Italy left the country's greatest film director inactive.

Nonetheless, Fellini managed to find a way to follow up his activity as a film director, a way to combine his two favorite means of expression—films and comic strips—so as not to give up creating images and to remain faithful to what he himself called "the dignity of keeping busy." He therefore accepted an invitation from the monthly comic magazine *Il Grifo*, its director Vincenzo Mollica, and his cartoonist friend Milo Manara to make comic strips of two of his unrealized (though never entirely abandoned) projects: *Viaggio a Tulum* and *Il viaggio di G. Mastorna* (Voyage to Tulum and The Voyage of G. Mastorna).

The *Viaggio a Tulum* was dreamed up by Fellini in 1984 and was inspired by the director's admiration for the work of the Peruvian anthropologist and writer Carlos Castaneda. The screenplay, co-written with Tullio Pinelli and published in installments in May 1986 in the national daily *Corriere della Sera*, began thus: "A film director, intrigued by the books of a Latin-American scholar which related stories, people, legends, and magical rites of the ancient Aztec peoples, has decided to base a film on them. In order to determine the feasibility of the project he arranges to meet the author, with the aim of traveling together to explore the settings of the writer's stories...." As for *Il viaggio di G. Mastorna* (a project that has since become legendary), this was supposed to be a film about self-acceptance and coming to terms with death. Conceived and written by Fellini in the summer of 1965 when he was distressed by the death of his dear friend, the Jungian analyst Ernest Bernhard, the film's realization was prevented by a chain of mishaps and setbacks, "bad vibrations," and bouts of illness.

The two projects were therefore transformed into *fumetti*, i.e., comic strips, which Fellini supervised with the utmost diligence and care. He discussed them with the artists and also suggested the "star" of the strip, the Italian comic actor Paolo Villaggio. He made studies for the makeup and costumes in a series of photographic sessions, and pasted them up in storyboard form, together with working drawings and sketches of details. Fellini carefully followed the emergence and evolution of these ideas and their successive transfer to print with the same creative commitment and scrupulousness he had devoted to film.

Of the original story that Fellini wrote for the cinema, very little remained in the film-comic strip first published in 1990 by Milano Libri-RCS; a second edition was issued in 1991 by Editori del Grifo with the title *Viaggio a Tulum. Milo Manara. Da un soggetto di Federico Fellini per un film da fare* (Voyage to Tulum. Milo Manara. From an Idea by Federico Fellini for a Film yet to be Made).

Vincenzo Mollica, the volume's editor, had this to say about the project: "What was at the beginning a relaxed and enjoyable supervision was transformed little by little into an authentic direction for the comic strip. The more we moved away from Fellini's original story, the more he created a new *Viaggio a Tulum*, full of fascinating inventions that took form thanks to the fine drawing skills of Milo Manara.... Fellini did not limit himself to suggesting situations and dialogues; he intervened—especially at the end—in the choice of frames, lighting angles, and characters' expressions."

These next pages contain examples of the work.

PER SIG. SHMIDERN
FAX 0474-73677
PER MILO MANARA

HERNANDEZ: O S. DIVERTE A

2.

pulviscolo
d'acqua

laghetto

HERNANDEZ:
QUESTO PULVISCOLO D'ACQUA
CHE BAGNI MI ACCAREZZA LA MIA FRONTE
MI SUSSURRA QUALCOSA ...

Luna
Silhouette
Hernandez
in retro

NARRATORE: COME TANTE PICCOLE CENTRALI
DI POTERE SPIRITUALE E
TRAMANDARE ALL'UMANITÀ
IGNORANTE E INFELICE
IL SENTIMENTO DI UNA
LIBERTÀ SENZA FINE.

8

DIDASCALIA: UNICA CHE PRENDE LO SUE VILLAGGIO
MA FORSE IL TEMPO
NON È ANCORA ARRIVATO
E I "NUOVI VEGGENTI"
DEPOSITARI DELL'ANTICA
CONOSCENZA VIVONO
IGNORATI E SCONOSCIUTI TRA DI NOI.

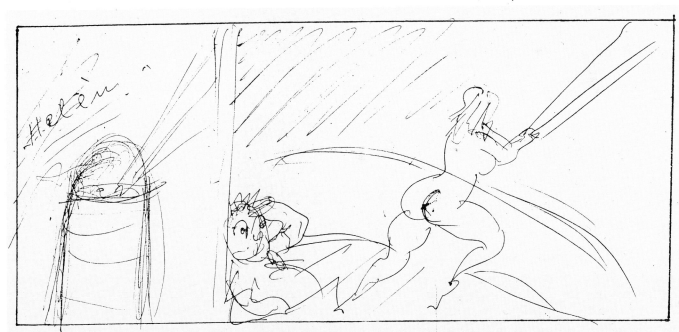

Mercedes li spalle
che continua a parlare
e davanti a lui
Suarez toga el
Emiliano che lo ascoltano

folla de passeggi
su una shala nottune
di una grande metropoli
europea

città americana
vista de sotto un
ponte dove sono
riuniti tri vagabondi

La Babel TOWER
con le vento aperte
e i fili degli squalori
e le sente Helen tutto
tremolare. Si intrepote
anche le nutte

Helen sforza un selva in
solta in preti nella balestra venento
in mano i fili degli squalori. Viennano
ha una mano nella vista come ti chi
si è svegliato di soprasalto

The film-comic strip *Il Viaggio di G. Mastorna detto Fernet* (The Voyage of G. Mastorna, called Fernet), published in 1992 in the monthly magazine *Il Grifo*, is a more famous version of unrealized Fellini work.

Its editor, Vincenzo Mollica, describes the working process: "After having written a short description, Fellini designed the story-board, precise and detailed, of the first part: indications of the countryside, the landscapes, the interiors, the furniture, the costumes, and—not least—the faces of the characters. He had not yet chosen the face for Mastorna.... After several changes of mind, his choice fell on Paolo Villaggio.... In order to give Manara, the artist who was drawing the strip, even more precise specifications, the director organized a photo session at Cinecittà, in which he made up Villaggio and then attempted to capture certain of the actor's expressions on film.... Fellini has used Manara's paint-brush exactly the same way he used lights with his director of photography.... and he has decided to elongate the title: to *Il viaggio di G. Mastorna* (G. stands for Giuseppe), he has added *detto Fernet*, which is a typical clown name."

On the following pages are examples from this work, including the opening note written by Fellini.

Io sarei il protagonista   di questa storia . Che faccia dovrebbe avere
un protagonista? Mi sarebbe tanto piaciuto avere una faccia come quella
di Edgar Allan poe,affascinante ~~misteriosa~~ *misteriosa* che ti strega solo
a guardarla.E tra gli attori? Jhon Barrymore, lo ricordate? Ecco quella
o Lawrence Olivier? no?
è una faccia da protagonista.Anche quella di Mastroianni mi sarebbe anda
mogani con dei
ta bene, ~~col~~ (baffetti,i capelli un pò ~~già~~ lunghi da artista.Invece io ho
una faccia così e me la tengo;anche se pensate che un protagonista do
vrebbe avere una faccia più importante,più carismatica, più *un emblematica.* ~~~~~~
forse   *pò*
Però posso esprimere ~~alcuni~~ esagerando un o quasi tutti i sentimenti ;
guardate;sbigottito, *o*
~~~~~~,la paura, arrabbiato, stupito,languido...strabico...
anche
Comunque con questa faccia non da protagonista mi è capitata ugualmente
nell'aereo che
un'avventura a dir poco eccezionale.Andiamo per ordine,~~~~~~~~~~~~~~
~~~~~~~~~~~~~~~~ mi riportava a casa dopo un lungo giro ~~nena~~
no *le capitali e nei paesi*
nel ~~~~~ del nord,mi stavo godendo un film con stanlio e Ollio.~~Che~~
meraviglioso
~~~~~~~~~~~~~~~~~~ pagliacci,quanto bene hanno fatto
all'umanità,che gioia poterli vedere e rivedere e sapere che ci sarann
per sempre.
~~Et to~~

Totale della pista. Tutti
in primo
poverina
... ecco si avvicina il momento! mi scoppia il cuore.
P. 17

E PERCHÉ NO. GLI APPLAUSI FANNO PARTE DELLA MIA VITA. SONO UNO CHE LAVORA ANCHE PER QUESTA SODDISFAZIONE. SONO... PRO... SCUSATE, MI SENTO UN PO' CONFUSO...

E' PIU' CHE NORMALE... SALIAMO SUL PULLMAN.

PREFERISCE LA SLITTA?

PREGO...

"My real occupation in life," observed Fellini, elegantly simplifying the complex processes behind his inspiration, "is to represent what I see, what kindles my imagination, what attracts or surprises me." In forty years, from 1950 when he co-directed *Luci del varietà* with Alberto Lattuada, to 1990, the year of his last film *La voce della luna*, Fellini co-directed one film, solo-directed another nineteen feature films, and filmed four shorts. In terms of quantity, that is neither many nor few. However, the overall legacy of Fellini's output is extraordinary, and no basic filmography could ever convey a proper idea of how much each film cost Fellini in human terms—the worries, expectations, incidents, and setbacks, the sheer difficulty in securing funds to finance his projects, the unpleasant and laborious deals, the constant obstacles, the frequent intolerable and even grotesque hardships faced by one of Europe's greatest twentieth-century film directors.

Many details have been taken from the book *I film di Federico Fellini* (published by Gremese), edited by Claudio G. Fava and Aldo Viganò, to whom we are very grateful.

Luci del varietà / Variety Lights
1950

Directors
Alberto Lattuada and Federico Fellini

Story
Federico Fellini

Screenplay
Federico Fellini, Alberto Lattuada, Tullio Pinelli
(with Ennio Flaiano)

Photography
Otello Martelli

Music
Felice Lattuada

Set Design
Aldo Buzzi

Editing
Mario Bonotti

Assistant Director
Angelo D'Alessandro

Director of Production
Bianca Lattuada

Executive Producer
Mario Ingrami

Producers
Alberto Lattuada, Federico Fellini

Production
Capitolium Film

Length
100 minutes

Cast
Carla Del Poggio (Liliana, Lilly Antonelli)
Peppino De Filippo (Checco Dalmonte)
Giulietta Masina (Melina Amour)
Folco Lulli (Adelmo Conti)
Franca Valeri (Hungarian choreographer)
Carlo Romano (Enzo La Rosa, attorney)
John Kitzmiller (John)
Silvio Bagolini (Bruno Antonini, reporter)
Dante Maggio (Remo, leader of theater company)
Alberto Bonucci & Vittorio Caprioli (stage duo)
Giulio Calì (fakir)
Mario De Angelis (maestro)
Checco Durante (theater owner)
Joe Fallotta (Bill)
Giacomo Furia (Duke)
Renato Malavasi (hotelier)
Fanny Marchiò (soubrette)
Gina Mascetti (Valeria Del Sole)
Vania Orico (gypsy singer)
Enrico Piergentili (Melina's father)
Marco Tulli (spectator)
Alberto Lattuada (theater assistant)

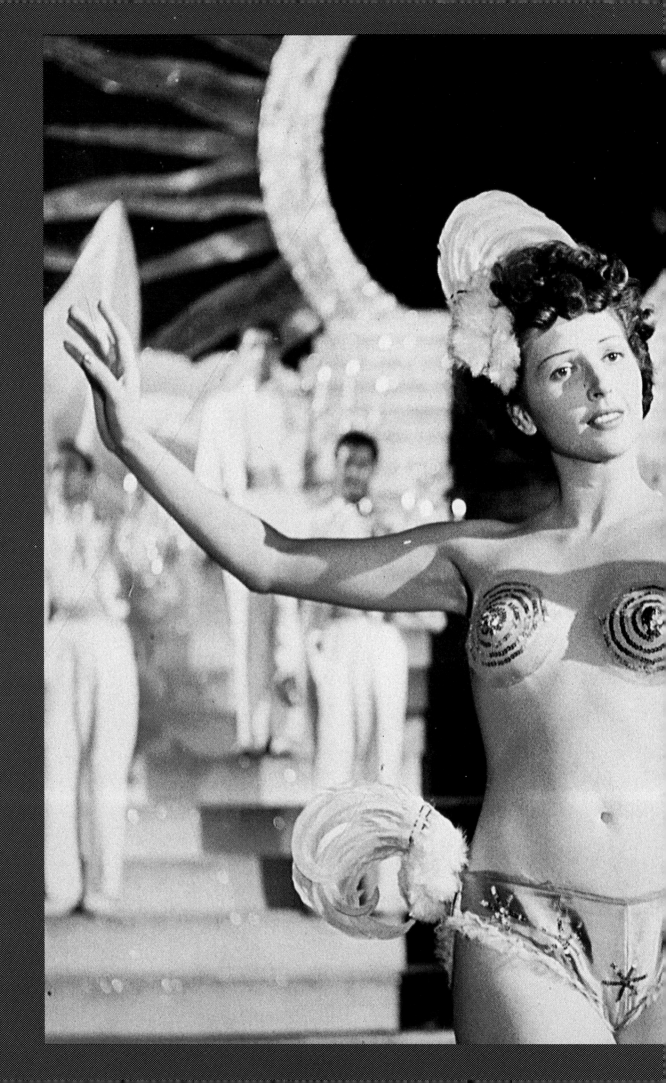

Lo sceicco bianco / The White Sheik

1952

Director
Federico Fellini

Story
Federico Fellini and Tullio Pinelli
(from an idea by Michelangelo Antonioni)

Screenplay
Federico Fellini, Tullio Pinelli
(with Ennio Flaiano)

Photography
Arturo Gallea

Music
Nino Rota

Set Design
Raffaello Tolfo

Editing
Rolando Benedetti

Assistant Director
Stefano Ubezio

Director of Production
Enzo Provenzale

Production Secretary
Renato Panetuzzi

Production
PDC-OFI

Length
85 minutes

Cast

Alberto Sordi (Fernando Rivoli, The White Sheik)
Brunella Bovo (Wanda Giardino Cavalli)
Leopoldo Trieste (Ivan Cavalli)
Giulietta Masina (Cabiria)
Lillia Landi (Felga)
Ernesto Almirante (photo-romance director)
Fanny Marchiò (Marilena Vellardi)
Gina Mascetti (White Sheik's wife)
Enzo Maggio (hotel porter)
Ettore M. Margadonna (Ivan's uncle)
Jole Silvani
Anna Primula
Nino Billi
Armando Libianchi
Ugo Attanasio
Elettra Zago
Giulio Moreschi
Piero Antonucci
Aroldino
Giorgio Salvioni
Antonio Acqua
Carlo Mazzoni
Rino Leandri
Guglielmo Leoncini

162

I vitelloni / I Vitelloni, The Young and Passionate
1953

Director
Federico Fellini

Story
Federico Fellini, Ennio Flaiano, Tullio Pinelli
(from an idea by Tullio Pinelli)

Screenplay
Federico Fellini, Ennio Flaiano

Photography
Otello Martelli, Luciano Trasatti, Carlo Carlini

Music
Nino Rota

Set Design
Mario Chiari

Costumes
Margherita Marinari Bomarzi

Editing
Rolando Benedetti

Assistant Directors
Moraldo Rossi, Franco Villa

Director of Production
Danilo Fallani

Production Secretary
Ugo Benvenuti

Production
Peg Film (Rome) / Cité Film (Paris)

Length
103 minutes

Cast
Franco Interlenghi (Moraldo)
Alberto Sordi (Alberto)
Franco Fabrizi (Fausto)
Leopoldo Trieste (Leopoldo)
Riccardo Fellini (Riccardo)
Eleonora Ruffo (Sandra)
Jean Brochard (Fausto's father)
Claude Farell (Alberto's sister)
Carlo Romano (antiques dealer)
Lida Baarova (dealer's wife)
Enrico Viarisio and Paola Borboni (Moraldo and Sandra's parents)
Arlette Sauvage (woman at movie)
Vira Silenti ('cinesina')
Maja Nipora (soubrette)
Achille Majeroni (theater company leader)
Silvio Bagolini (fool)
Giovanna Galli
Franca Gandolfi
Gondrano Trucchi
Guido Martufi
Milvia Chianelli
Gustavo De Nardo
Graziella De Roc

"Agenzia matrimoniale" / "A Marriage Agency"
1953

Director
Federico Fellini

Story
Federico Fellini

Screenplay
Federico Fellini, Tullio Pinelli

Photography
Gianni Di Venanzo

Music
Mario Nascimbene

Set Design
Gianni Polidori

Editing
Eraldo Da Roma

Assistant Director
Luigi Vanzi

Producer
Cesare Zavattini

Production
Faro Film

Length
32 minutes

Cast
Antonio Cifariello (reporter)
Livia Venturini (Rossana)
non-professional actors

Fourth episode from *L'Amore in città / Love in the City* (issue no. 1 of
the film magazine *Lo Spettatore*, edited by Cesare Zavattini, Riccardo
Ghione, Marco Ferreri).

174

La strada / La Strada
1954

Director
Federico Fellini

Story
Federico Fellini, Tullio Pinelli

Screenplay
Federico Fellini, Tullio Pinelli
(with Ennio Flaiano)

Photography
Otello Martelli

Music
Nino Rota

Set Design
Mario Ravasco

Costumes
Margherita Marinari Bomarzi

Editing
Leo Catozzo

Assistant Director
Moraldo Rossi

Artistic Collaboration
Brunello Rondi

Director of Production
Luigi Giacosi

Executive Producers
Danilo Fallani, Giorgio Morra, Angelo Cittadini

Production
Dino De Laurentiis, Carlo Ponti

Length
94 minutes

Cast
Giulietta Masina (Gelsomina)
Anthony Quinn (Zampanò)
Richard Basehart (Matto 'The Fool')
Aldo Silvani (Signor Giraffa)
Marcella Rovere (The Widow)
Livia Venturini (The Sister)
Mario Passante
Yami Kamedeva
Anna Primula

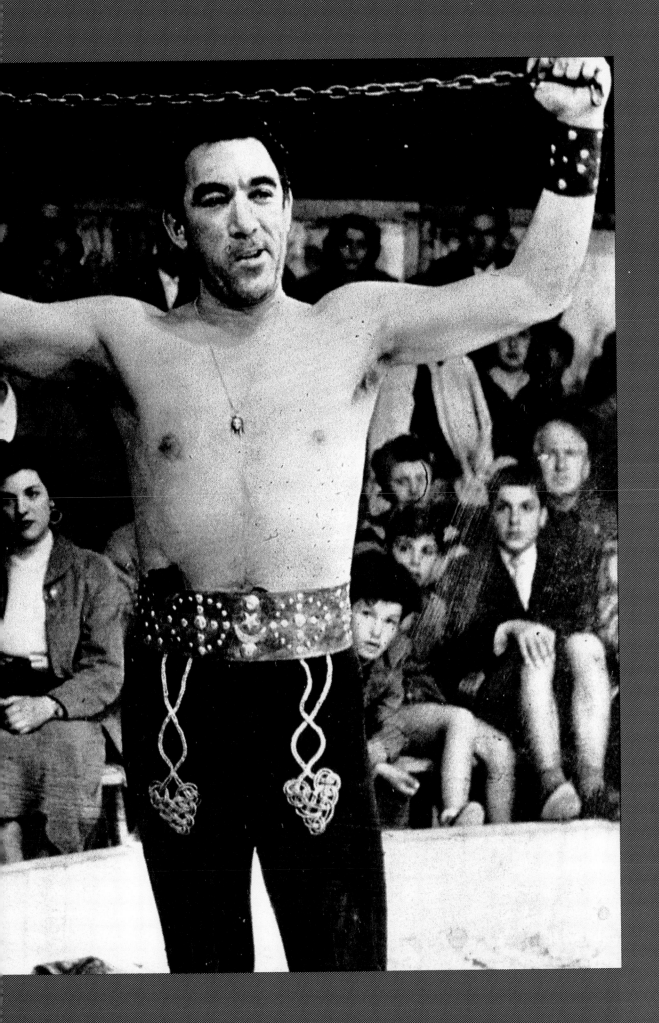

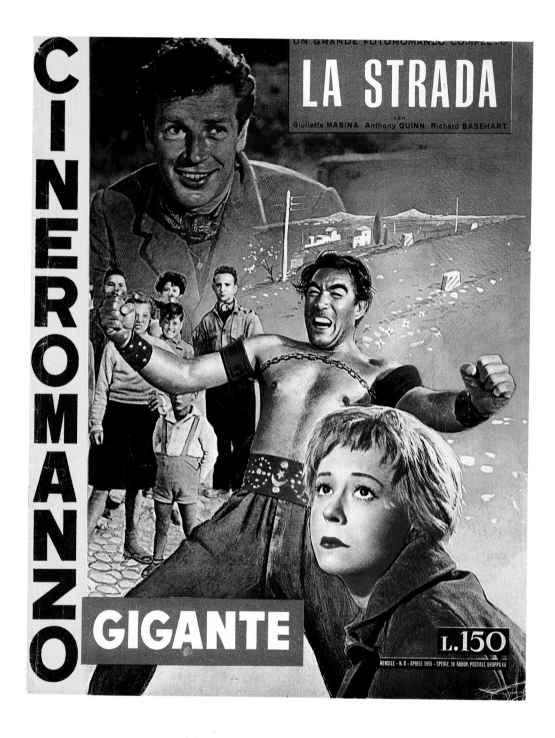

Il bidone / The Swindle
1955

Director
Federico Fellini

Story and Screenplay
Federico Fellini, Ennio Flaiano, Tullio Pinelli
(from an idea by Federico Fellini)

Photography
Otello Martelli

Music
Nino Rota

Set Design and Costumes
Dario Cecchi

Editing
Mario Serandrei, Giuseppe Vari

Assistant Directors
Moraldo Rossi, Narciso Vicario

Artistic Collaboration
Brunello Rondi

Director of Production
Giuseppe Colizzi

Production Secretary
Manolo Bolognini

Production
Titanus (Rome) / SGC (Paris)

Length
104 minutes

Cast
Broderick Crawford (Augusto)
Richard Basehart (Picasso)
Franco Fabrizi (Roberto)
Giulietta Masina (Iris)
Giacomo Gabrielli (Vargas)
Alberto De Amicis (Rinaldo)
Sue Ellen Blake (Susanna)
Lorella De Luca (Patrizia)
Mara Werlen (dancer)
Xenia Valderi
Mario Passante
Irene Cesaro
Riccardo Garrone
Paul Grenter
Emilio Manfredi
Lucetta Muratori
Sara Simoni
Maria Zanoli
Ettore Bevilacqua
Ada Colangeli
Amedeo Trilli
Tiziano Cortini
Gino Buzzanca
Rosanna Fabrizi
Barbara Varenna
Yami Kamedeva
Gustavo De Nardo
Gianna Cobelli
Tullio Tomadoni
Grazia Carini
Giuliana Manoni

Le notti di Cabiria / The Nights of Cabiria
1957

Director
Federico Fellini

Story and Screenplay
Federico Fellini, Ennio Flaiano, Tullio Pinelli
(from an idea by Federico Fellini)

Dialogue Co-writer
Pier Paolo Pasolini

Artistic Collaboration
Brunello Rondi

Photography
Aldo Tonti

Music
Nino Rota

Set Design and Costumes
Piero Gherardi

Editing
Leo Catozzo

Assistant Directors
Moraldo Rossi, Dominique Delouche

Director of Production
Luigi De Laurentiis

Production Secretary
Narciso Vicario

Production
Dino De Laurentiis (Rome) / Les Films Marceau (Paris)

Length
110 minutes

Cast
Giulietta Masina (Cabiria)
François Périer (Oscar D'Onofrio)
Franca Marzi (Wanda)
Dorian Gray (Jessy)
Amedeo Nazzari (Alberto Lazzari)
Aldo Silvani (fakir)
Mario Passante (lame man)
Pina Gualandri (Matilda)
Polidor (friar)
Ennio Girolami (pimp)
Christian Tassou
Jean Molier
Riccardo Fellini
Maria Luisa Rolando
Amedeo Girard
Loretta Capitoli
Mimmo Poli
Giovanna Gattinoni

Un film di DINO DE LAURENTIIS
distribuito dalla Paramount

Paramount
GUIDA
PUBBLICITARIA

GIULIETTA MASINA · AMEDEO NAZZARI
nel film

NC 1

Le notti di Cabiria

La dolce vita / La Dolce Vita
1960

Director
Federico Fellini

Story
Federico Fellini, Tullio Pinelli, Ennio Flaiano
(from an idea by Federico Fellini)

Screenplay
Federico Fellini, Tullio Pinelli, Ennio Flaiano

Co-screenwriter
Brunello Rondi

Photography
Otello Martelli

Music
Nino Rota

Set Design and Costumes
Piero Gherardi

Makeup
Otello Fava

Editing
Leo Catozzo

Assistant Directors
Guidarino Guidi, Paolo Nuzzi, Dominique Delouche

Director's Assistants
Gianfranco Mingozzi, Giancarlo Romani, Lilli Veenman

Directors of Production
Manlio M. Moretti, Nello Meniconi

Production Secretaries
Mario Basile, Mario De Biase, Osvaldo De Micheli

Production
Riama Film (Rizzoli-Amato, Rome) /
Pathé Consortium Cinéma (Paris)

Length
178 minutes

Marcello Mastroianni (Marcello Rubini)
Anita Ekberg (Sylvia)
Anouk Aimée (Maddalena)
Yvonne Furneaux (Emma)
Alain Cuny (Steiner)
Annibale Ninchi (Marcello's father)
Laura Betti (Laura)
Magali Noël (Fanny)
Valeria Ciangottini (Paola)
Franca Pasutt (girl covered with feathers)
Renée Longarini (Signora Steiner)
Walter Santesso (Paparazzo)
Adriana Moneta (prostitute)
Giulio Paradisi (second photographer)
Enzo Cerusico (third photographer)
Enzo Doria (fourth photographer)
Leonardo Botta (doctor)
Harriet White (Sylvia's secretary)
Carlo Di Maggio (Totò Scalise, producer)
Lex Barker (Robert)
Sandy von Norman (press conference interpreter)
Adriano Celentano (rock'n'roll singer)
Gio Staiano (effeminate youth)
Archie Savage (black dancer)
Giacomo Gabrielli (Maddalena's father)
Gianfranco Mingozzi (priest in church with Steiner)
Rina Franchetti (mother of lying miracle children)
Marianne Leibl (woman with Emma at the miracle)
Giulio Questi (Giulio Mascalchi)
Audrey McDonald (Sonia)
Nico Otzak (girl in Via Veneto)
Ferdinando Brofferio (Maddalena's lover)
Doris Pignatelli (lady with the white collar)
Franco Rossellini (riding instructor)
Giulio Girola (police commissioner)
Giuliana Lojodice (the Steiners' maid)
Sandra Lee (ballerina at Spoleto)
Jacques Sernas (matinée idol)
Polidor and Iris Tree
Leonida Repaci
Anna Salvatore
Letizia Spadini
Margherita Russo
Desmond O'Grady
Winie Vagliani
Francesco Luzi
Francesco Consalvo
Wadim Wolkonsky
Eugenio Ruspoli
Ivenda Dobrzensky
Ida Galli
Mario De Grenet
Cristina Paolozzi
Elisabetta Cini
Brunoro Serego Alighieri
Mino Doro
Antonio Jacono
Carlo Musto
Daniela Calvino
Umberto Orsini
Renato Mambor

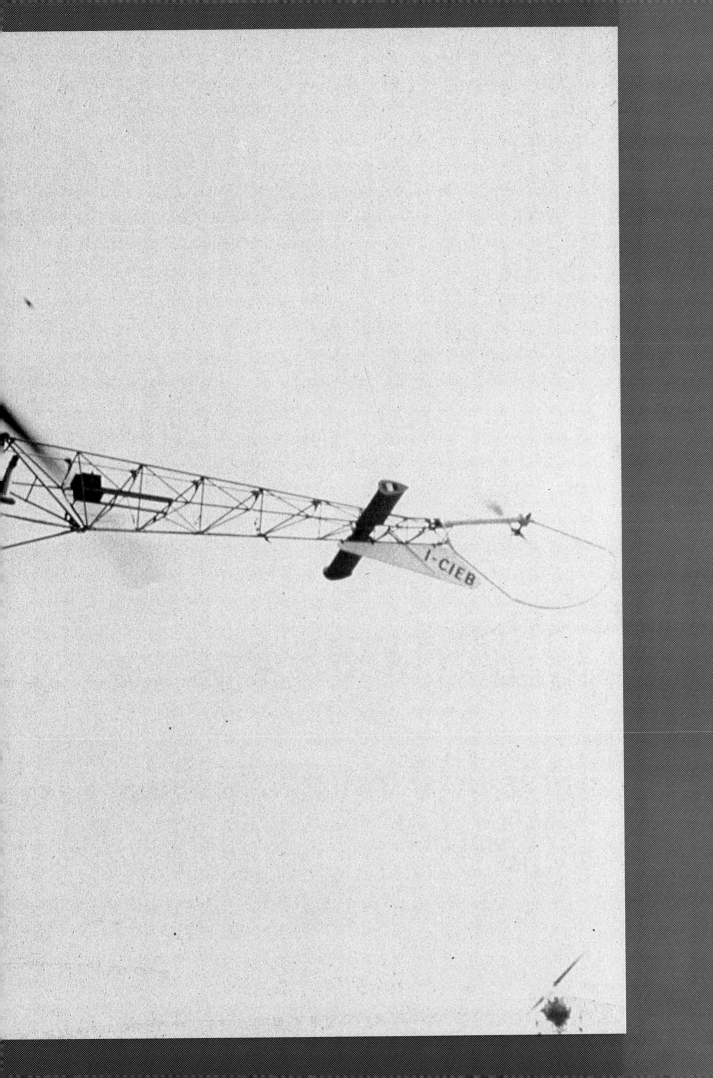

a Walter Santesso
"Paparazzo"

Birth of an absolute image
Rome, summer 1958: for fun
the photographer Pierluigi
Praturlon takes a series of
shots of his friend Anita Ekberg
prancing about in the Trevi
Fountain, published later in the
weekly *Tempo Illustrato*.
Fellini saw the photos (printed
here together with a shot of the
photographer dancing with the
barefoot Anita in an antique-
style night club in Rome), which
gave him the inspiration
for one of the most
widely known scenes from
La Dolce Vita, providing an
indelible symbol for the entire film.

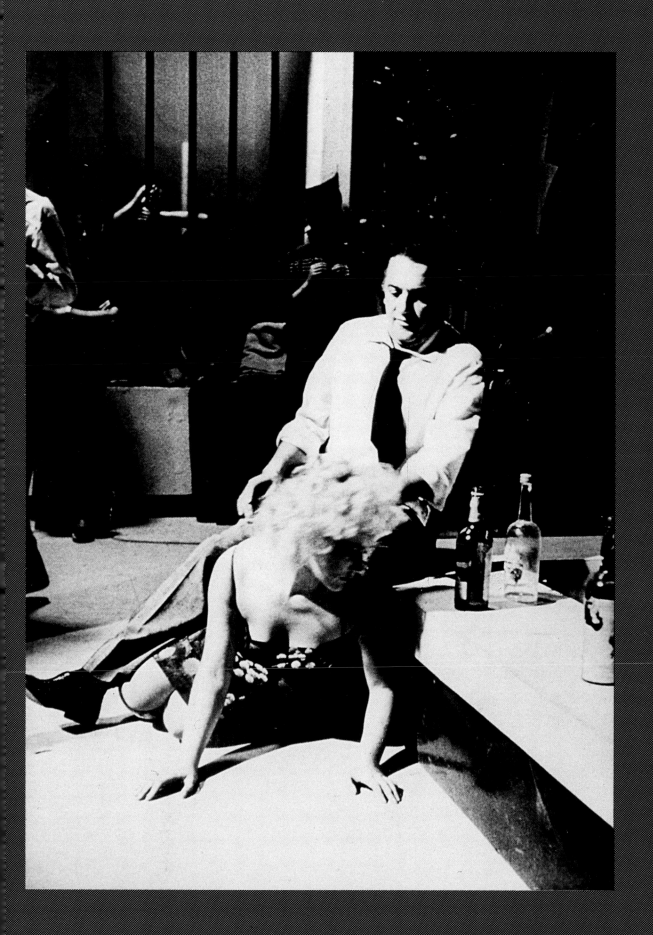

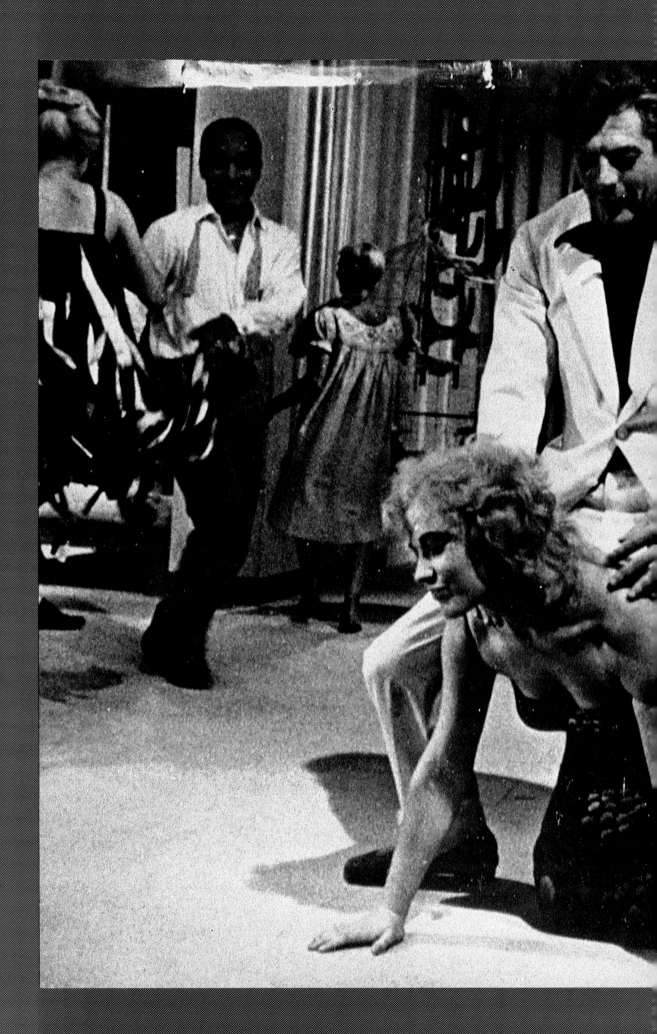

"Le tentazioni del dottor Antonio" / "The Temptations of Dr. Antonio"
1962

Director
Federico Fellini

Story
Federico Fellini

Screenplay
Federico Fellini, Tullio Pinelli, Ennio Flaiano
(with Brunello Rondi and Goffredo Parise)

Photography
Otello Martelli

Music
Nino Rota

Set Design
Piero Zuffi

Editing
Leo Catozzo

Executive Producer
Carlo Ponti

Production
Concordia Compagnia Cinematografica
and Cineriz (Rome), Francinex and Gray Films (Paris)

Length
60 minutes

Peppino De Filippo (Dr. Antonio Mazzuolo)
Anita Ekberg (woman in poster)
Antonio Acqua (police commissioner)
Eleonora Nagy (the child)
Dante Maggio and Donatella Della Nora (sisters of Dr. Antonio)
Giacomo Furia
Alfredo Rizzo
Alberto Sorrentino
Monique Berger
Polidor
Mario Passante
Silvio Bagolini
Achille Majeroni
Enrico Ribulsi
Gesa Meiken
Gondrano Trucchi
Ciccio Bardi
Giulio Paradisi

Second episode of Cesare Zavattini's
Boccaccio '70.
Other episodes: 'Renzo e Luciana' by Mario Monicelli,
'Il Lavoro' by Luchino Visconti,
'La Riffa' by Vittorio De Sica

8 1/2 - 8 1/2
1963

Director
Federico Fellini

Story
Federico Fellini, Ennio Flaiano
(from an idea by Federico Fellini)

Screenplay
Federico Fellini, Tullio Pinelli, Ennio Flaiano
Brunello Rondi

Photography
Gianni Di Venanzo

Music
Nino Rota

Set Design and Costumes
Piero Gherardi

Editing
Leo Catozzo

Assistant Directors
Guidarino Guidi, Giulio Paradisi, Francesco Aluigi

Artistic Collaboration
Brunello Rondi

Makeup
Otello Fava

Director of Production
Nello Meniconi

Executive Producers
Clemente Fracassi, Alessandro von Norman

Production Secretary
Albino Morandin

Production
Cineriz (Rome) / Francinex (Paris)

Length
114 minutes

Cast
Marcello Mastroianni (Guido Anselmi)
Anouk Aimée (Luisa, Guido's wife)
Sandra Milo (Carla)
Claudia Cardinale (Claudia)
Rossella Falk (Rossella)
Barbara Steel (Gloria)
Guido Alberti (Pace, the producer)
Mario Pisu (Mezzabotta)
Madeleine Lebeau (French actress)
Jean Rougeul (Daumeri, the critic)
Caterina Boratto (woman at spa)
Annibale Ninchi (Guido's father)
Giuditta Rissone (Guido's mother)
Edra Gale (Saraghina)
Mario Conocchia (Director of Production)
Cesarino Miceli Picardi (Production Supervisor)
Tito Masini (cardinal)
Jacqueline Bonbon (soubrette)
Jan Dallas (Maurice, the magician)
Georgia Simmons (Guido's grandmother)
Edy Vessel (Edy, striptease artist)
Annie Gorassini (Pace's friend)
Rossella Como (Luisa's companion)
Elisabetta Catalano (Luisa's sister)
Gilda Dahlberg (American journalist's wife)
Olimpia Cavalli (Olimpia)
Hazel Rogers (black girl)
Bruno Agostini (Production Secretary)
Mino Doro (Claudia's agent)
Mario Tarchetti (Claudia's press agent)
Polidor (clown)
Mark Herron (Luisa's admirer)
Enrico Cini
Sebastiano De Leandro
Frazier Rippy
Roberta Valli
Eva Gioia
Dina De Santis
Roby Nicolosi
Neil Robinson
Eugene Walter
Mary Indovino
John Stacy
Francesco Rigamonti
Matilde Calman
Alfredo De Lafeld
Marisa Colomber
Maria Raimondi
Nadine Sanders
Riccardo Guglielmi
Marco Gemini
Giulio Calì

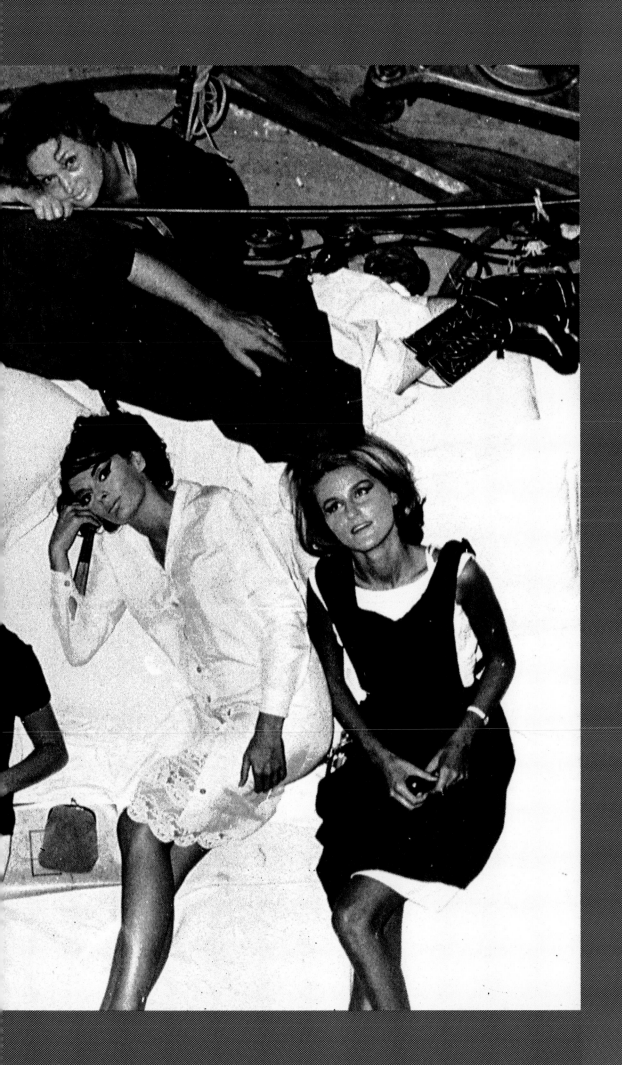

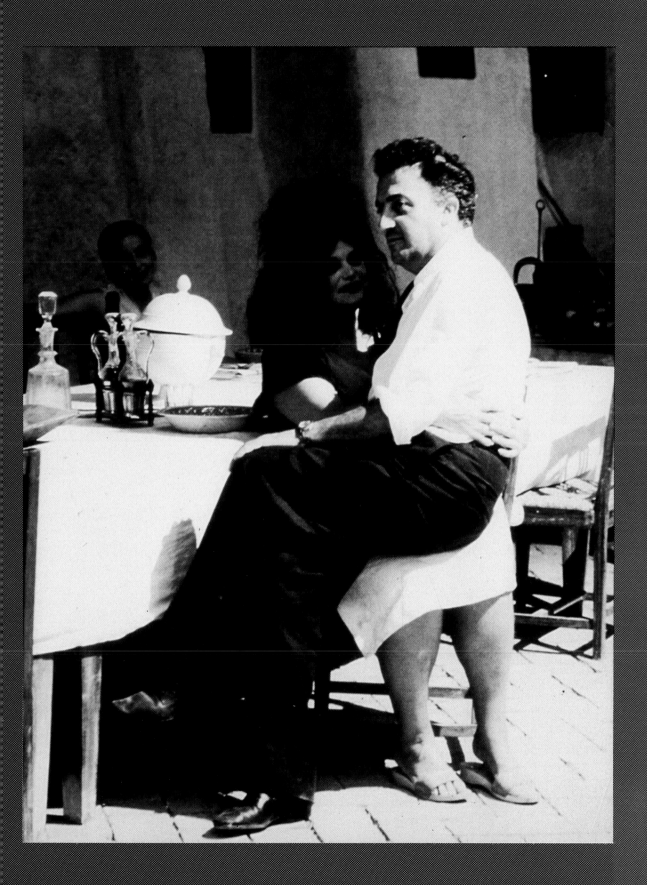

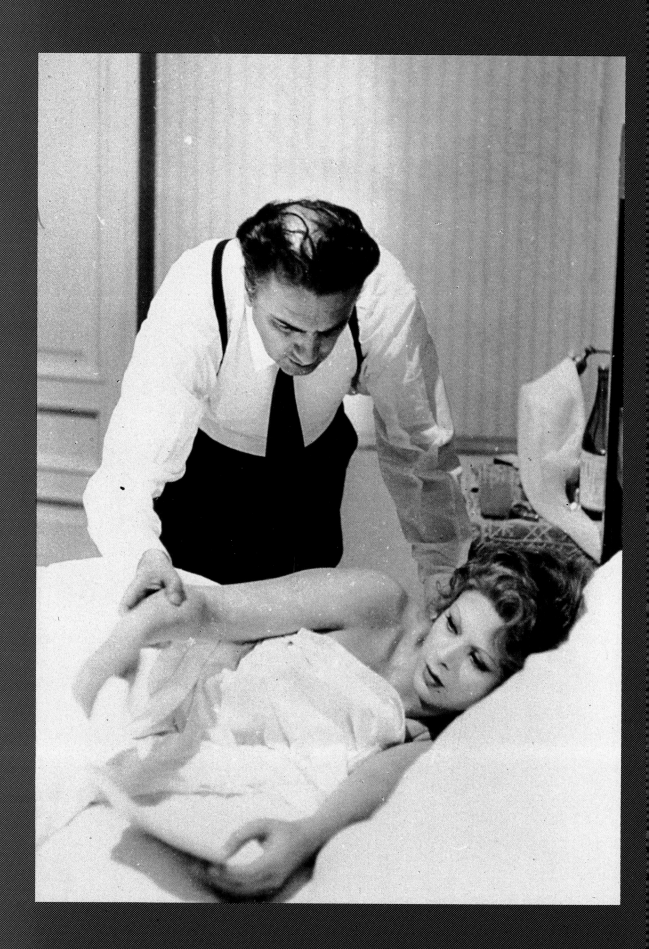

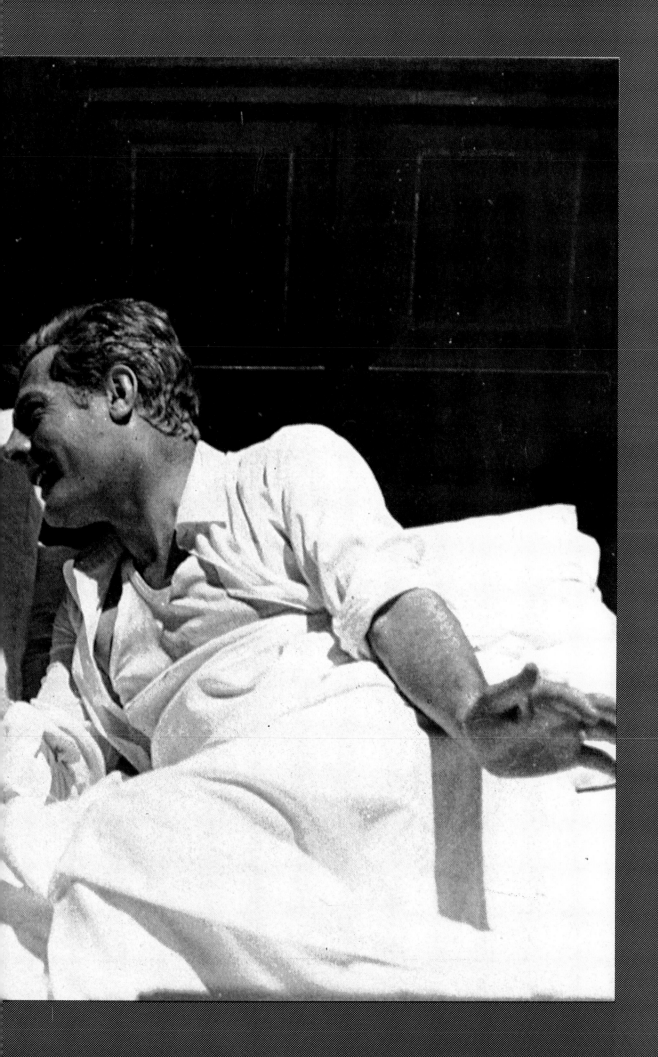

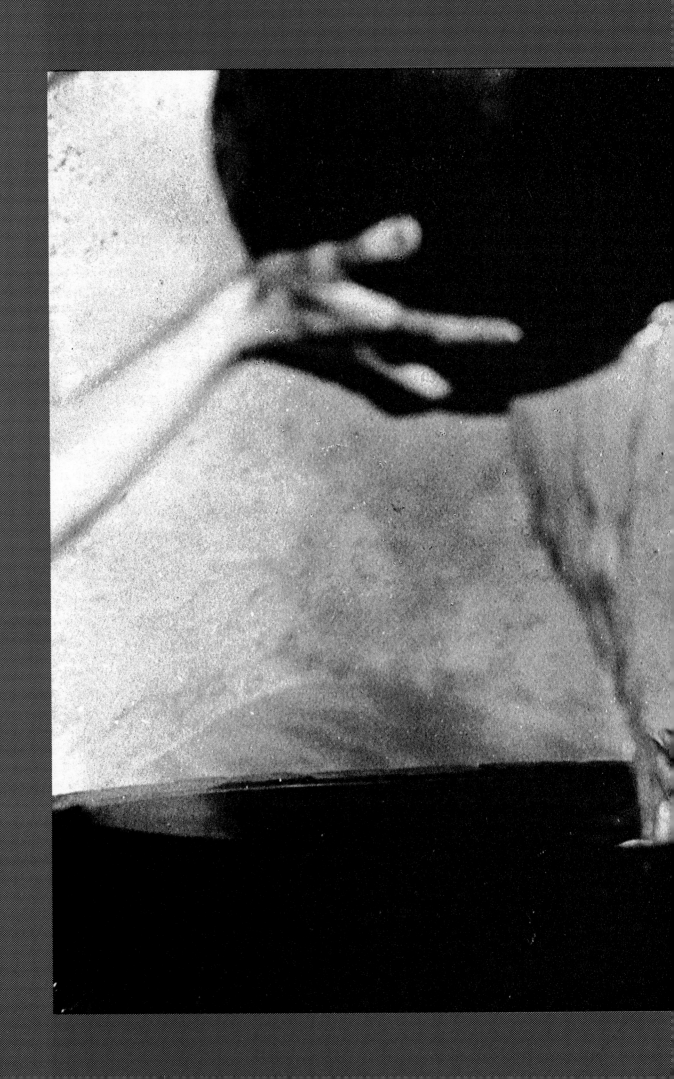

238

Giulietta degli spiriti / Juliet of the Spirits
1965

Director
Federico Fellini

Story
Federico Fellini, Tullio Pinelli
(from an idea by Federico Fellini)

Screenplay
Federico Fellini, Tullio Pinelli, Ennio Flaiano

Co-screenwriter
Brunello Rondi

Photography
Gianni Di Venanzo

Music
Nino Rota

Set Design and Costumes
Piero Gherardi

Editing
Ruggero Mastroianni

Assistant Directors
Francesco Aluigi, Liliana Betti, Rosalba Zavoli

Makeup
Otello Fava

Directors of Production
Mario Basili, Alessandro von Norman

Production Secretaries
Renato Fié, Ennio Onorati

Executive Producer
Clemente Fracassi

Production
Federiz (Rome) / Francoriz (Paris)

Length
129 minutes

Giulietta Masina (Giulietta Boldrini)
Mario Pisu (Giorgio, Giulietta's husband)
Sandra Milo (Susy, Iris, Fanny)
Valentina Cortese (Valentina)
Caterina Boratto (Giulietta's mother)
Lou Gilbert (Giulietta's grandfather)
Sylvia Koscina and Luisa Della Noce (Giulietta's sisters)
José de Villalonga (Giulietta's admirer)
Valeska Gert (medium)
Silvana Jachino (Dolores)
Fred Williams (Arab prince)
Milena Vukotic (Giulietta's house maid, the saint)
Frederich Lebedur (school head, guru)
Anne Francine (psychoanalyst)
Elena Fondra (Elena)
Elisabetta Gray (Giulietta's second maid)
Genius (Genius, medium)
Dany Paris (Susy's desperate friend)
Alberto Plebani
Yvonne Casadei
Mario Conocchia
Cesarino Miceli Picardi
Felice Fulchignoni
Lia Pistis
Alba Cancellieri
Dina De Santis
Hildegarde Golex
Walter Harrison
Asoka and Sujata Rubener
Bill Edwards
Elena Cumani
Gianni Bertoncin
Federico Valli
Giorgio Grillo Rufino
Remo Risaliti
Giorgio Ardisson
Nadir Moretti
Alba Rosa
Bob Edwards
Alberto Cevenini
Selyna Seyn
Jacqueline Gerard
Anita Sanders
Wanani
Jacques Herlin
Robert Walders
Guido Alberti
Mino Doro
Raffaele Guida
Alicia Brandet
Mary Arden
Sabrina Gigli
Rossella Di Sepio
Irina Alexeieva
Alessandra Mannoukine
Gilberto Galvan
Edoardo Torricella
Massimo Sarchielli

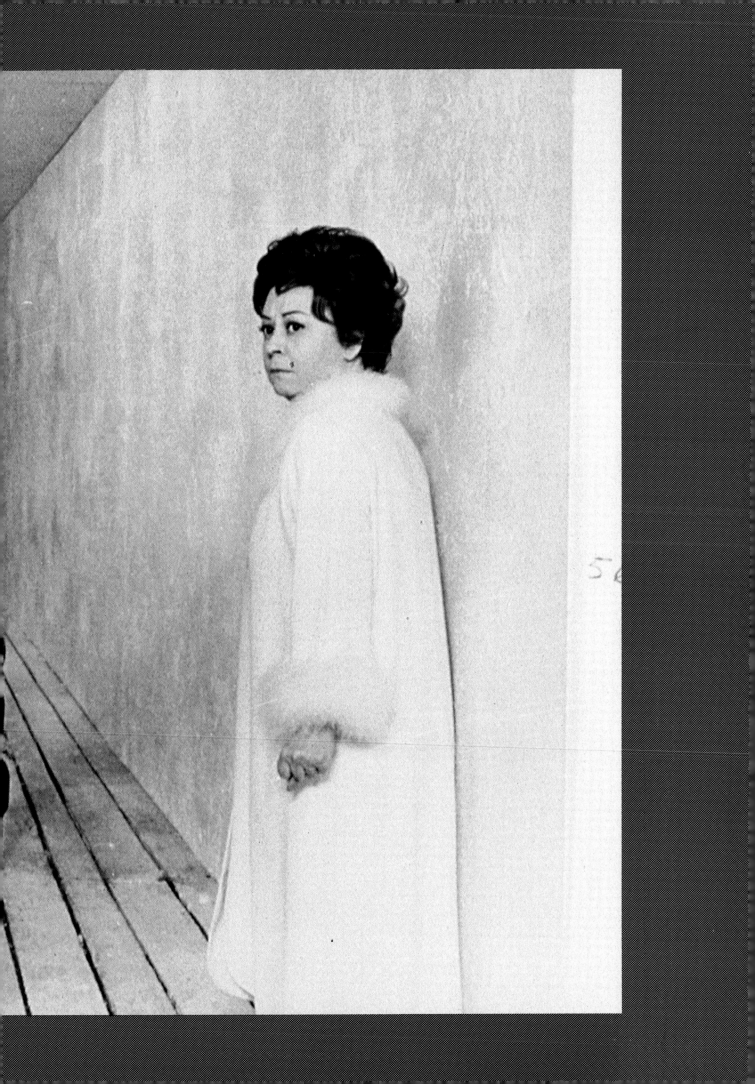

"Toby Dammit" / "Toby Dammit"
1968

Director
Federico Fellini

Story
free adaptation of the short story
"Never Bet the Devil Your Head"
by Edgar Allan Poe

Screenplay
Federico Fellini, Bernardino Zapponi

Photography
Giuseppe Rotunno

Music
Nino Rota

Set Design and Costumes
Piero Tosi

Editing
Ruggero Mastroianni

Assistant Directors
Eschilo Tarquini, Francesco Aluigi, Liliana Betti

Director of Production
Tommaso Sagone

Executive Producer
Enzo Provenzale

Producers
Alberto Grimaldi, Raymond Eger

Production
PEA (Rome) / Les Films Marceau (Paris)
Cocinor (Paris)

Length
37 minutes

Cast
Terence Stamp (Toby Dammit)
Salvo Randone (Father Spagna)
Antonia Pietrosi (actress)
Polidor (old actor)
Anne Tonietti (TV commentator)
Fabrizio Angeli (first director)
Ernesto Colli (second director)
Aleardo Ward (first interviewer)
Paul Cooper (second interviewer)
Marina Yaru (little girl)
Marisa Traversi
Rick Boyd
Mimmo Poli
Brigitte

Third episode from the film *Tre passi nel delirio / Histoires
Extraordinaires / Spirits of the Dead.*
Other episodes: 'Metzengerstein' by Roger Vadim;
'William Wilson' by Louis Malle.

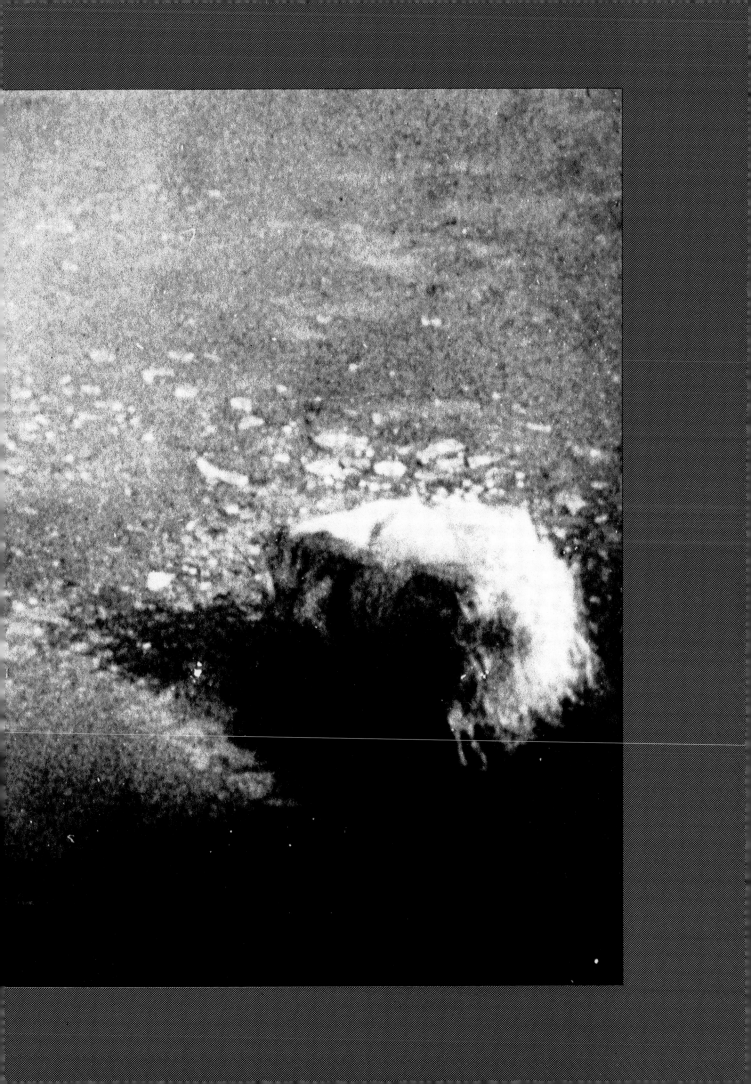

Block-notes di un regista /
A Director's Notebook
1969

Director
Federico Fellini

Story and Screenplay
Federico Fellini, Bernardino Zapponi

Photography
Pasquale De Santis

Music
Nino Rota

Editing
Ruggero Mastroianni

Assistant Directors
Maurizio Mein, Liliana Betti

Executive Producer
Lamberto Pippia

Producer
Peter Goldfarb

Production
NBC (USA)

Length
60 minutes

Cast   255
(as themselves)
Federico Fellini
Giulietta Masina
Marcello Mastroianni
Caterina Boratto
Marina Boratto
David Mauhsell
Genius
Cesarino
Gasparino
Bernardino Zapponi
Lina Alberti
non professional actors

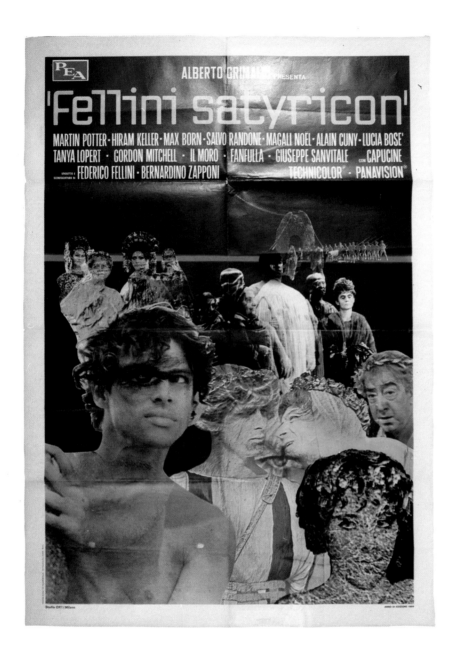

Fellini Satyricon / Fellini's Satyricon
1969

Director
Federico Fellini

Story
free adaptation of Petronius's *Satyricon*

Screenplay
Federico Fellini, Bernardino Zapponi

Photography
Giuseppe Rotunno

Music
Nino Rota, with Ilhan Mimaroglu,
Tod Docksader, Andrew Rudin

Set Design and Costumes
Danilo Donati, Luigi Scaccianoce
(concepts by Federico Fellini)

Editing
Ruggero Mastroianni

Makeup
Rino Carboni

Assistant Director
Maurizio Mein

Director's Assistants
Liliana Betti, Lia Consalvo

Director of Production
Roberto Cocco

Executive Producer
Enzo Provenzale

Production Secretary
Michele Pesce

Production Supervisors
Lamberto Pippia, Gilberto Scarpellini, Fernando Rossi

Producer
Alberto Grimaldi

Production
PEA (Rome) /
Les Productions Artistes Associés (Paris)

Length
138 minutes

Cast
Martin Potter (Encolpius)
Hiram Keller (Ascyltus)
Max Born (Gitone)
Salvo Randone (Eumolpo)
Mario Romagnoli (Trimalchio)
Magali Noël (Fortunata)
Capucine (Triphena)
Alain Cuny (Lica)
Fanfulla (Vernacchio)
Danika La Loggia (Scintilla)
Giuseppe Sanvitale (Abinna)
Genius (Libertus)
Lucia Bosé (suicidal woman)
Joseph Wheeler (suicide)
Tanya Lopert (emperor)
Gordon Mitchell (robber)
Luigi Montefiori (Minotaur)
Marcello Di Falco (proconsul)
Elisa Mainardi (Arianna)
Donyale Luna (Enotea)
Carlo Giordana (ship's captain)
Pasquale Baldassarre (hermaphrodite)

FEDERICO FELLINI

I CLOWNS

I clowns / The Clowns
1970

Director
Federico Fellini

Story and Screenplay
Federico Fellini, Bernardino Zapponi

Photography
Dario Di Palma

Music
Nino Rota

Set Design and Costumes
Danilo Donati, Renzo Gronchi

Editing
Ruggero Mastroianni

Assistant Director
Maurizio Mein

Makeup
Rino Carboni

Director's Assistant
Liliana Betti

Director of Production
Lamberto Pippia

Producers
Elio Scardamaglia, Ugo Guerra

Production
RAI (Italy) / ORTF (France) / Bavaria Film (Germany) /
Compagnia Leone Cinematografica

Length
93 minutes

Cast
(as themselves)
Liana, Rinaldo, Nando Orfei
Franco Migliorini
Anita Ekberg
(as the clowns)
Billi
Scotti
Fanfulla
Reder
Valentini
Merli
Rizzo
Pistoni
Furia
Sbarra
Carini
Terzo
Vingelli
Fumagalli
Zerbinati
the Colombaioni
the Martana
Maggio
Janigro
Mausell
Peverello
Sorrentino
Valdemaro
Bevilacqua
(as members of the troupe)
Maya Morin
Lina Alberti
Alvaro Vitali
Gasparino
(as the French clowns)
Alex
Bario
Père Loriot
Ludo
Charlie Rivel
Maiss
Nino
(as themselves)
Pierre Etaix
Victor Fratellini
Baptiste & Tristan Remy
Pipo & Rhum
Buglioni
Hugue

Roma / Fellini's Roma
1972

Director
Federico Fellini

Story and Screenplay
Federico Fellini, Bernardino Zapponi

Photography
Giuseppe Rotunno

Music
Nino Rota

Set Design and Costumes
Danilo Donati, concept by Federico Fellini

Editing
Ruggero Mastroianni

Assistant Director
Maurizio Mein

Director's Assistants
Paolo Pietrangeli, Tonino Antonucci

Makeup
Rino Carboni

Director of Production
Lamberto Pippia

Production Supervisors
Alessandro Gori, Fernando Rossi, Alessandro Sarti

Executive Producer
Danilo Marciani

Production
Ultra Film (Rome) / Les Productions Artistes Associés
(Paris)

Length
119 minutes

Cast
Peter Gonzales (Fellini at 18)
Fiona Florence (prostitute)
Marne Maitland (guide in the catacombs)
Galliano Sbarra and Alvaro Vitali (curtain raiser
presenters at the Teatro Jovinelli)
Norma Giacchero (Mastroianni interviewer)
Federico Fellini (himself)
(as themselves)
Britta Barnes
Pia De Doses
Renato Giovannoli
Elisa Mainardi
Paule Rouf
Paola Natale
Marcelle Ginette Bron
Mario Del Vago
Alfredo Adami
Stefano Majore
Gudrun Mardou
Giovanni Serboli
Angela De Leo
Libero Frissi
Dante Cleri
Mimmo Poli
Marcello Mastroianni
Anna Magnani
Gore Vidal
John Francis Lane
Alberto Sordi

FRANCO CRISTALDI

PRESENTA

FEDERICO FELLINI
AMARCORD

SOGGETTO E SCENEGGIATURA DI
FEDERICO FELLINI E TONINO GUERRA

IL LIBRO OMONIMO E' EDITO IN ITALIA DA
RIZZOLI

UNA COPRODUZIONE ITALO-FRANCESE
F.C. (ROMA) P.E.C.F. (PARIGI)

PRODOTTO DA
FRANCO CRISTALDI

REGIA DI
FEDERICO FELLINI

TECHNICOLOR ®

UNA ESCLUSIVITA' P.I.C.

Amarcord / Amarcord
1973

Director
Federico Fellini

Story and Screenplay
Federico Fellini, Tonino Guerra
(from an idea by Federico Fellini)

Photography
Giuseppe Rotunno

Music
Nino Rota

Set Design and Costumes
Danilo Donati (concept by Federico Fellini)

Editing
Ruggero Mastroianni

Assistant Director
Maurizio Mein

Director's Assistants
Liliana Betti, Gérard Morin, Mario Garriba

Makeup
Rino Carboni

Director of Production
Lamberto Pippia

Production Supervisors
Alessandro Gori, Gilberto Scarpellini

Production Secretaires
Fernando Rossi, Giuseppe Bruno Bossio

Producer
Franco Cristaldi

Production
FC Produzioni (Rome) / PECF (Paris)

Length
127 minutes

Cast
Bruno Zanin (Titta Biondi)
Pupella Maggio (Miranda, Titta's mother)
Armando Brancia (Aurelio, Titta's father)
Stefano Proietti (Oliva, Titta's brother)
Giuseppe Ianigro (Titta's grandfather)
Nandino Orfei (Titta's uncle)
Carla Mora (Carla, housemaid)
Ciccio Ingrassia (mad uncle)
Magali Noël (Gradisca)
Luigi Rossi (attorney)
Maria Antonietta Belussi (tobacconist)
Josiane Tanzilli (Volpina)
Domenico Pertica (blind man of Cantarel)
Antonio Faà di Bruno (count)
Carmela Eusepi (count's daughter)
Gennaro Ombra (Biscein)
Gianfilippo Carcano (Don Balosa)
Aristide Caporale (Giudizio)
Francesco Maselli
Dina Adorni
Francesco Vona
Lino Patruno
Armando Villella
Francesco Magno
Gianfranco Marrocco
Fausto Signoretti
Donatella Gambini
Fides Stagni
Fredo Pistoni
Ferruccio Brambilla
Antonio Spaccatini
Marcello Di Falco
Bruno Scagnetti
Alvaro Vitali
Ferdinando De Felice
Mario Silvestri
Dante Cleri
Mario Liberati
Marina Trovalusci
Fiorella Magalotti
Vincenzo Caldarola
Mario Milo
Cesare Martignoni
Mario Jovinelli
Costantino Serraino
Amerigo Castrichella
Dario Giacomelli
Giuseppe Papaleo
Mario Nebolini
Bruno Bartocci
Clemente Baccherini
Torindo Bernardo
Marcello Bonini Olas
Marco Laurentino
Riccardo Satta

Il Casanova di Federico Fellini / Fellini's Casanova
1976

Director
Federico Fellini

Story
free adaptation of Giacomo Casanova's autobiographical
"Storie della mia vita" (Story of My Life)

Screenplay
Federico Fellini, Bernardino Zapponi

Photography
Giuseppe Rotunno

Music
Nino Rota

Set Design and Costumes
Danilo Donati (concept by Federico Fellini)

Editing
Ruggero Mastroianni

Assistant Directors
Maurizio Mein, Liliana Betti, Gérard Morin

Makeup
Rino Carboni (Giannetto De Rossi
for Donald Sutherland's makeup)

Executive Producer
Giorgio Morra

Director of Production
Lamberto Pippia

Production Assistants
Alessandro von Norman, Maria Di Biase

Production Secretaries
Titti Pesaro, Luciano Bonomi

Producer
Alberto Grimaldi

Production
PEA (Rome)

Length
170 minutes

Cast
Donald Sutherland (Giacomo Casanova)
Tina Aumont (Henriette)
Cicely Brown (Marchioness of Urfé)
Carmen Scarpitta and Diane Kourys (Mesdames Charpillon)
Clara Algranti (Marcolina)
Margareth Clementi (Sister Maddalena)
Daniela Gatti (Giselda)
Mario Cencelli (entomologist)
Olimpia Carlisi (Isabella, the entomologist's daughter)
Silvana Fusacchia (his other daughter)
Chesty Morgan (Barberina)
Adele Angela Lojodice (mechanical doll)
Sandra Elaine Allen (giant lady)
Clarissa Mary Roll (Anna Maria)
Alessandra Belloni (princess)
Marika Rivera (Astrodi)
Angelica Hansen (hunchback actress)
Marijorie Bell (Countess Waldenstein)
Marie Marquet (Casanova's mother)
Daniel Emilfork-Berenstein
Luigi Zerbinati
Hans Van Den Hoek
Dudley Sutton
John Karlsen
Reggie Nalder
Vim Hiblom
Harold Innocent
Misha Bayard
Nicolas Smith
Donald Hodson
Dan Van Husen
Gabriele Carrara
Marcello Di Falco
Sara Pasquali
Mariano Brancaccio
Veronica Nava
Carli Buchanan
Mario Gagliardo

Prova d'orchestra / Orchestra Rehearsal
1979

Director
Federico Fellini

Story
Federico Fellini

Screenplay
Federico Fellini, with Brunello Rondi

Photography
Giuseppe Rotunno

Music
Nino Rota

Set Design
Dante Ferretti

Costumes
Gabriella Pescucci

Editing
Ruggero Mastroianni

Assistant Director
Maurizio Mein

Director's Assistants
Christa Reeh, Giovanni Bentivoglio

Executive Producer
Lamberto Pippia

Production
Daime Cinematografica S.p.A. and RAI-TV (Rome) /
Albatros Produktion GmbH (Munich)

Length
70 minutes

Cast
Baldwin Bass (conductor)
Clara Colosimo (harpist)
Elisabeth Labi (pianist)
Ronaldo Bonacchi (contrabassoon player)
Ferdinando Villella (cellist)
Giovanni Javarone (tuba player)
David Mauhsell (first violinist)
Francesco Aluigi (second violinist)
Andy Miller (oboe player)
Sybil Mostert (flautist)
Franco Mazzieri (trumpeter)
Daniele Pagani (trombone player)
Luigi Uzzo (violinist)
Cesare Martignoni (clarinetist)
Umberto Zuanelli (copyist)
Filippo Trincia (orchestra secretary)
Claudio Ciocca (union leader)
Angelica Hansen and Heinz Kreuger (violinists)
Federico Fellini (interviewer's voice)

La città delle donne / City of Women
1980

Director
Federico Fellini

Story and Screenplay
Federico Fellini, Bernardino Zapponi
(with Brunello Rondi)

Photography
Giuseppe Rotunno

Music
Luis Bacalov

Set Design
Dante Ferretti (concept by Federico Fellini)

Costumes
Gabriella Pescucci

Editing
Ruggero Mastroianni

Assistant Directors
Maurizio Mein; Jean Louis Godfroy for the second unit

Director's Assistants
Giovanna Bentivoglio, Franco Amurri

Executive Producer
Lamberto Pippia

Directors of Production
Francesco Orefici, Philippe Lorain Bernard

Producer
Franco Rossellini

Production
Opera Film (Rome) / Gaumont (Paris)

Length
145 minutes

Cast   313
Marcello Mastroianni (Snàporaz)
Anna Prucnal (Snàporaz's wife)
Bernice Stegers (woman on the train)
Ettore Manni (Katzone)
Iole Silvani (motorcyclist)
Donatella Damiani (soubrette)
Alessandra Panelli (housewife with child)
Hélène G. Calzarelli
Catherine Carrel
Marcello Di Falco
Silvana Fusacchia
Gabriella Giorgelli
Dominique Labourier
Stephane Emilfork
Sylvie Mayer
Meerberger Nahyr
Sibilla Sedat
Katrin Gebeleink
Nadia Vasil
Loredana Solfizi
Fiorella Molinari
Rosaria Tafuri
Sylvie Waerenier
Carla Terlizzi
Jill and Viviane Lucas
Mara Ciukleva
Mimmo Poli
Nello Pazzafini
Armando Parracino
Umberto Zuanelli
Pietro Fumagalli

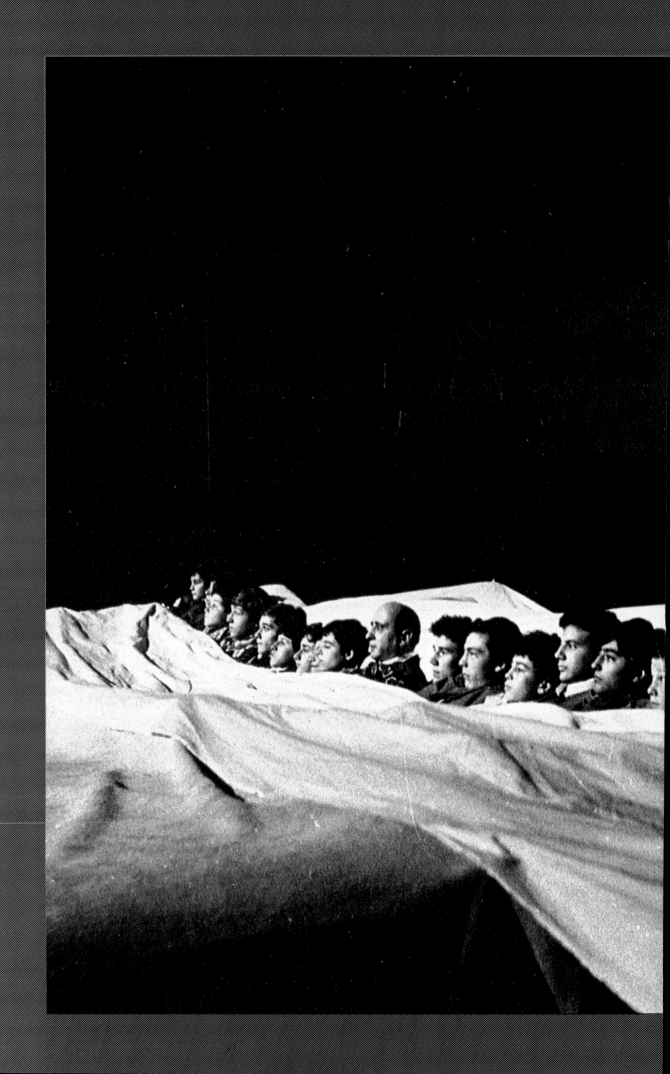

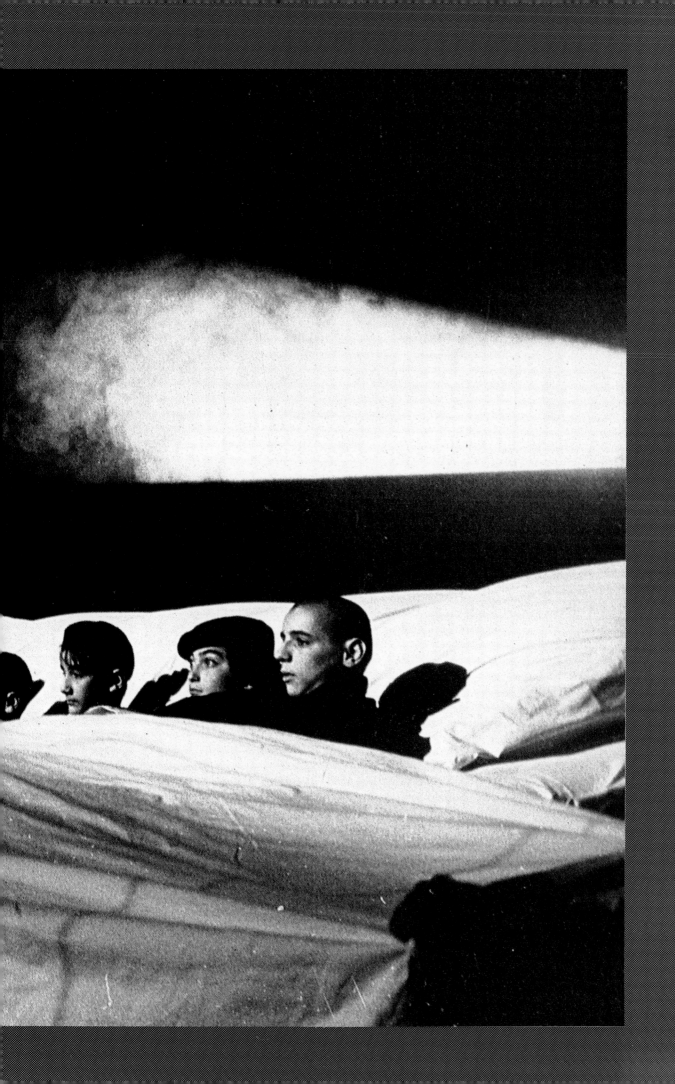

E la nave va / And the Ship Sails On
1983

Director
Federico Fellini

Story and Screenplay
Federico Fellini, Tonino Guerra; Andrea Zanzotto
(opera lyrics)

Photography
Giuseppe Rotunno

Music
Gianfranco Plenizio

Set Design
Dante Ferretti

Costumes
Maurizio Millenotti

Editing
Ruggero Mastroianni

Assistant Director
Gianni Arduini

Director's Assistant
Andrea De Carlo

Executive Producer
Piero Notarianni

Director of Production
Lucio Orlandini

Producer
Franco Cristaldi

Associate Producer
Aldo Nemni

Production
RAI/Vides Produzione (Rome) / Gaumont (Paris)

Length
132 minutes

Cast
Freddie Jones (Orlando)
Barbara Jefford (Ildebranda Cuffari)
Victor Poletti (Aureliano Fuciletto)
Peter Cellier (Sir Reginald Dongby)
Elisa Mainardi (Teresa Valegnani)
Norma West (Lady Violet Dongby)
Paolo Paoloni (Maestro Albertini)
Sarah Jane Varley (Dorotea)
Fiorenzo Serra (Grand-Duke)
Pina Bausch (Princess Lherimia)
Pasquale Zito (Count Bassano)
Janet Suzman (Edmea Tetua)
Lina Polan (Ines Ruffo Saltini)
Philip Locke (Prime Minister)
Jonathan Cecil (Ricotin)
Maurice Barrier (Ziloev)
Fred Williams
Elizabeth Kaza
Colin Higgins
Vittorio Zarfait
Umberto Zuanelli
Ugo Frangareggi
Claudio Ciocca
Antonio Vezza
Alessandro Partexano
Domenica Pertica
Christian Fremont
Marielle Duvelle
Helen Stirling

Ginger e Fred / Ginger and Fred
1985

Director
Federico Fellini

Story
Federico Fellini, Tonino Guerra

Screenplay
Federico Fellini, Tonino Guerra, Tullio Pinelli

Photography
Tonino Delli Colli, Ennio Guarnieri

Music
Nicola Piovani

Set Design
Dante Ferretti

Costumes
Danilo Donati

Editing
Nino Baragli, Ugo De Rossi, Ruggero Mastroianni

Assistant Director
Gianni Arduini

Director's Assistants
Filippo Ascione, Daniela Barbiani, Eugenio Cappuccio,
Anke Zindler

Executive Producer
Luigi Millozza

Directors of Production
Walter Massi, Gianfranco Coduti, Roberto Mannoni,
Raymond Leplont

Producer
Alberto Grimaldi

Production
PEA (Rome) / REVCOM Films, Les Films Ariane,
FR3 Films Production (Paris), Stella Film,
Anthea (Munich) in collaboration with RAI-Uno (Italy)

Length
125 minutes

Cast
Giulietta Masina (Ginger)
Marcello Mastroianni (Fred)
Franco Fabrizi (television presenter)
Frederick Ledenburg (admiral)
Augusto Pederosi (transvestite)
Martin Maria Blau (assistant director)
Jacques Henri Lartigue (flying friar)
Toto Mignone (Toto)
Ezio Marano (intellectual)
Antoine Saint-Jean (assistant)
Frederiek Tun (kidnappee)
Antonio Iuorio (TV inspector)
Barbara Scoppa (reporter)
Salvatore Billa (Clark Gable)
Ginestra Spinola (mother)
Stefania Marini (TV secretary)
Francesco Casale (Mafia hood)
Gianfranco Alpestre (attorney)
Filippo Ascione (pianist)
Elena Cantarone (nurse)
Cosima Chiusoli (wife of defrocked priest)
Alessandro Partexano (sailor)
Leonardo Petrillo (Marcel Proust)
Renato Grilli (Franz Kafka)
Daniele Aldovrandi (Marty Feldmann)
Barbara Golinska (Marlene Dietrich)
Luigi Duca (Adriano Celentano)
Eolo Capritti (Kojak)
Nadia Giallorenzo (Queen Elisabeth II)
Carlo di Placido (Ronald Reagan)
Fabrizio Libralesco (Woody Allen)
Claudio Ciocca
Sergio Ciulli
Federica Paccosi
Tiziana Bucarella
Elena Magola
Mauro Misul
Franco Trevisi
Narciso Vicario
Vittorio De Bisogno
Roberto De Sandro
Fabrizio Fontana
Laurentina Guidotti
Giorgio Iovine
Danika La Loggia
Isabelle-Thérèse La Porte
Luigi Leoni
Luciano Lombardo
Marielle Loreley
Franco Marino
Jurgen Morhofer
Pippo Negri
Antonietta Patriarca
Nando Pucci Negri
Patty Vailati
Herman Weiskoff

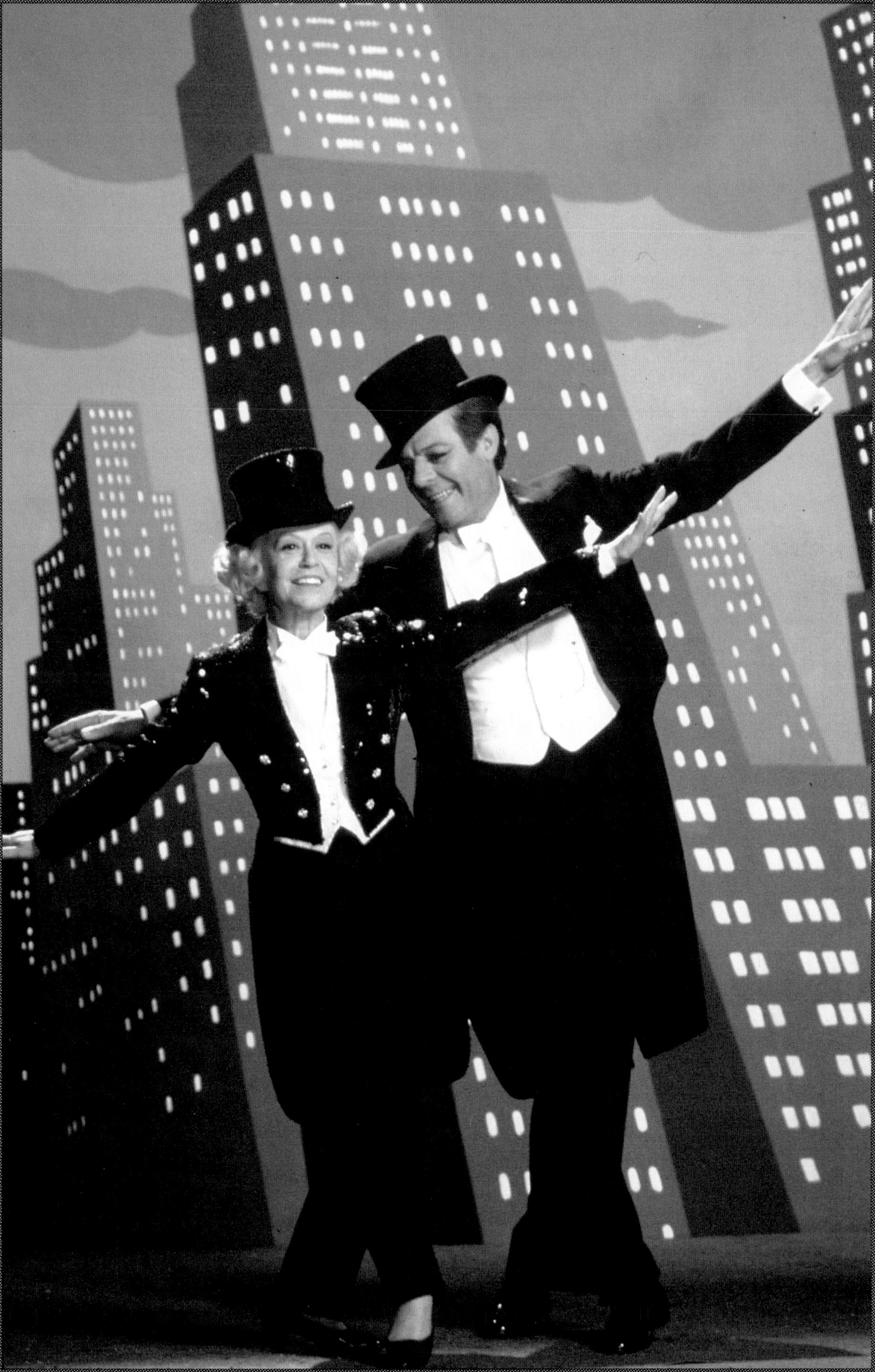

Intervista / Interview
1987

Director
Federico Fellini

Screenplay
Federico Fellini, Gianfranco Angelucci

Photography
Tonino Delli Colli

Music
Nicola Piovani

Set Design and Costumes
Danilo Donati

Editing
Nino Baragli

Production Supervisor
Michele Janczarek

Executive Producer
Pietro Notarianni

Production
Aljosha Production (Ibrahim Moussa) / RAI-Uno / Cinecittà

Length
105 minutes

Cast
(as themselves)
Federico Fellini
Marcello Mastroianni
Anita Ekberg
Sergio Rubini (reporter)
Maurizio Mein (assistant director)
Lara Wendel (newlywed)
Paola Liguori (matinée idol)
Nadia Ottaviani (custodian of Cinecittà)
Antonella Ponziani (girl)

La voce della luna / The Voice of the Moon
1990

Director
Federico Fellini

Story
free adaptation of the novel "Il poema dei lunatici"
by Ermanno Cavazzoni

Screenplay
Federico Fellini, Tullio Pinelli, Ermanno Cavazzoni

Photography
Tonino Delli Colli

Music
Nicola Piovani

Set Design
Dante Ferretti

Costumes
Maurizio Millenotti

Editing
Nino Baragli

Production
Mario and Vittorio Cecchi Gori, for C.G. Group
Tiger-Cinemax, in collaboration with RAI (Rome)

Length
118 minutes

Cast
Roberto Benigni (Ivo Salvini)
Paolo Villaggio (the Prefect Gonnella)
Nadia Ottaviani (Aldina Ferruzzi)
Marisa Tomasi ('steam locomotive')
Sim (oboe player)
Susy Blady (Aldina's sister)
Angelo Orlando (Nestore)
Dario Ghirardi (reporter)
Dominique Chevalier (Tazio Micheluzzi)
Nigel Harris (Giuanin Micheluzzi)
Eraldo Turra (attorney)
Giordano Falzoni (teacher)
Ferruccio Brambilla (doctor)
Giovanni Javarone (grave-digger)
Lorose Keller (Duchess)
Patrizio Roversi (the Prefect's son)

"Time seems to be standing still," remarked Fellini on his seventieth birthday. "I feel as if I came into the world at the age of twenty-two or twenty-three, and that nothing else has happened to me since. From the very first day on the set, I never left it—I've continued doing the same things. The years have just crept by, one after the other, imperceptibly, as in a very long film."

He was right. The first part of his biography brims with events, encounters, trips back and forth, activities and facts; the second part is taken up entirely by his film work: a concentrated, methodical existence typical of many a great artist and master creator.

Many items of information have been taken from the book *Fellini* (published by Camunia), an excellent biography by the Italian film critic Tullio Kezich, to whom we are most grateful.

A family portrait
His mother Ida Barbiani
Newborn baby Federico
With his brother Riccardo in 1926

1920

Born in Rimini on January 20, under the sign of Capricorn (with ascendant in Virgo), to Ida Barbiani, housewife, and Urbano Fellini, sales representative.

Soon after will come a brother, Riccardo, born February 27, 1921, actor; and a sister, Maddalena, born October 17, 1929, housewife and actress.

1925

Starts school at the San Vincenzo kindergarten in Rimini; the following year he moves on to the Carlo Tonini state school.

He is a quiet child who loves drawing, playing with miniature theaters and puppets; soon develops a passion for the comic strips in the *Corriere dei Piccoli*, a weekly supplement to one of the national dailies: his favorite strip is the one by Antonio Rubino.

With his brother Riccardo
Both wearing the 'avant-garde'
uniform of the Fascist youth
organization, Rimini, 1933

With his father Urbano and brother
Riccardo in Venice, 1937
At a family get-together, 1938
(second-to-last from right)

1930

Attends the Giulio Cesare elementary school; in the eight school years that follow, his inseparable classmate is Luigi Benzi, known as "Titta," who would remain a lifelong friend.

1936

Falls in love with his next-door neighbor, the fourteen-year-old Bianca Soriani; though Bianca leaves Rimini two years later, the two continue to see each other and correspond by letter for some time afterward.

Caricatures signed *Fellas* drawn
for the portrait studio
launched in Rimini with
his painter friend Demos Bonini
under the banner
FEBO (Fellini-Bonini), 1937

Caricatures of American movie stars
(Joel McCrea, Herbert Marshall)
for the billboards outside
the Fulgor, in Rimini, 1937

1937

Publishes his first drawings: a set of caricatures depicting some of the
participants of a summer camp run by the Verrucchio branch of the
Fascist Party, in which Fellini took part the previous year; the draw-
ings appear in the only issue of *La Diana*, published by the Opera
Nazionale Balilla (Fascist youth organization) under the title of
"Campeggisti 1936" (Campers of 1936). The entries are signed "Av.
Federico Fellini" ("Av." stands for "avant-garde").

Commissioned by the manager of the Fulgor movie theater in Rimini
to create a set of caricatures of well-known actors, to use on the billboards.

Opens a little portrait workshop for vacationers together with his
painter friend Demos Benini, and gives it the name "FEBO" (Fellini-
Benini).

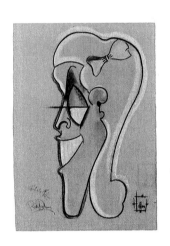

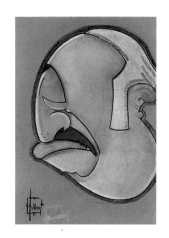

In the Rome radio studios
of the EIAR (Ente Italiano
Audizioni Radiofoniche), 1940

1938

Passes his final exams and is admitted to high school.

Publishes cartoons in the weekly supplement *La Domenica del Corriere* in the column reserved for reader contributions. Offers to join the team working on the Florence-based satirical magazine *420* run by the publisher Nerbini; from then on his short stories, columns, comic strips, and drawings become regular features, all signed "Fellas." This continues through 1939.

1939

Moves with his mother and sister to Rome; they return to Rimini a year later to rejoin his father and brother. Then brother Riccardo moves to Rome.

Enrolls at the Faculty of Law, Rome University; does not finish his degree.

Becomes acquainted with the painter Rinaldo Geleng, a friendship that would last a lifetime.

Begins to work frenetically on *Marc'Aurelio*, a highly successful bi-weekly review of political satire, published by Rizzoli; achieves growing recognition for his comic strips, short stories in installments, and feature series (among those particularly successful with younger readers were "Ma tu mi stai a sentire?"; "Luci della città"; "Seconda liceo"; "Primo amore"). His contributions to the review continue through the end of 1942.

Meets and befriends the comic actor Aldo Fabrizi through friend Ruggero Maccari, and becomes the actor's gag writer and creator of material for variety shows and film roles.

Manages to avoid the draft using various excuses (heart problems, Basedow's disease) and in fact never joins the army.

1940

On June 10 Italy enters the world conflict, declaring war on France and England.

Begins working on the radio (EIAR, Ente Italiano Audizioni Radiofoniche) with radio reviews, sketches, shows, "fantasies," and humorous stories, often paired with his friend Ruggero Maccari; the job continues through to the end of the summer of 1943. Also contributes to a variety of periodicals, including film magazines.

Participates officially in his first playscript as a gag writer for the film *Il pirata sono io!*, directed by Mario Mattoli, starring the comedian Erminio Macario.

Caricature of Nino Za

Cartoons by Fellini for
the humorous Roman biweekly
Marc'Aurelio, 1940–41

Potenza della suggestienza

— Che fai Decio?
— Ti dò un becio.

(dis. di Federico)

Tutti e due

— Io mangio sempre in trattoria a
prezzo fisso...
— Anche io voglio conservare la
linea... (dis. di Federico)

Presentazione tra analfabeti

(dis. di Federico)

1941   Co-writes the screenplay of *Documento Z-3*, directed by Alfredo
Guarini, starring Isa Miranda and Claudio Gora.

1942

Meets Giulia Masina, a young stage actress who is also one of the
EIAR's comic actors for "Terziglio," a radio show focused on the
daily adventures of a young married couple, Cico and Pallina (with
scripts by Fellini). The two young artists meet, fall in love, and get
engaged.

Writes the storyline and co-scripts the film *Avanti c'è posto*, directed
by Mario Bonnard, starring Aldo Fabrizi. With Piero Tellini, writes
the storyline for the film *Quarta pagina*, directed by Nicola Manzari.
Works for a brief spell in the scripts office of the A.C.I. (Alleanza
Cinematografica Italiana), a body set up by Benito Mussolini's son
Vittorio; meets director Roberto Rossellini here.

Has his first try behind the camera in Tripoli, Africa, when he is
asked to stand in as emergency director on a film for which he himself
had written the story, *Gli ultimi Tuareg* or *I cavalieri del deserto*; the
film troupe is called back suddenly to Rome, where the British army
is on the point of occupying the city.

Invitation drawn by Fellini
for his wedding to Giulietta Masina
in Rome, October 30, 1943,
celebrated in a neighbor's
apartment, Monsignor Cornaggia
Medici officiating

357

1943

Co-writes screenplays for the films *Campo de' Fiori*, directed by Mario Bonnard (which sees the first joint appearance of Aldo Fabrizi and Anna Magnani, who would later star together in *Roma città aperta*, directed by Roberto Rossellini); *Apparizione*, directed by Jean De Limur and starring Alida Valli and Amedeo Nazzari; *L'ultima carrozzella*, directed by Mario Mattoli and starring Aldo Fabrizi and Anna Magnani; *Chi l'ha visto?*, directed by Goffredo Alessandrini and starring Virgilio Riento and Valentina Cortese.

Flees to the house in Rome where Giulietta Masina lives with an aunt. The Fascist government falls on July 25, and Mussolini with it. On September 8 the king flees the capital and escapes to the south, which is already in the hands of Anglo-American troops. Both the center and the north of the country remain in the grip of the Nazis; the Fascists declare the foundation of the Italian Social Republic.

Marries Giulietta Masina on October 30 in a private ceremony with a select group of guests in the apartment of their next-door neighbor, Monsignor Cornaggia Medici, who is authorized to conduct the rite even outside the church. That afternoon the newlyweds slip off to the Galleria movie theater, where the star of the curtain raiser, Alberto Sordi, points the couple out among the audience, to great applause from all.

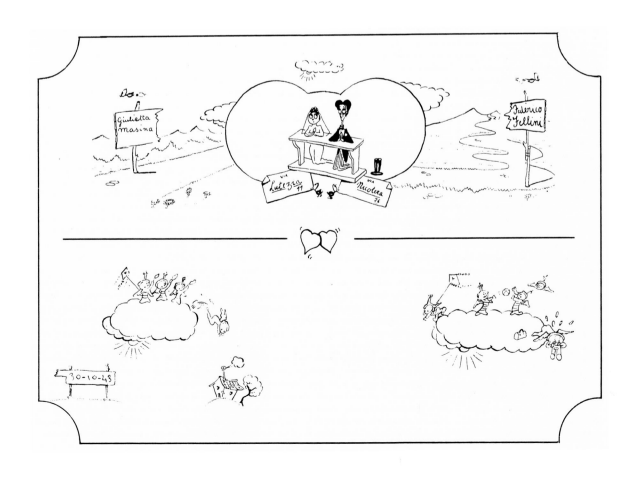

Outside one of the Roman
caricature studios frequented by
Allied servicemen, 1944
Two of Fellini's cartoons
of this period

1944

Opens The Funny Face Shop just after the liberation of Rome (on June 4) by the Allied forces, with a group of comic-strip writers, including De Seta, Verdini, Camerini, Scarpelli, Majorana, Guasta, Giobbe, Attalo, and Migneco. Here they work for the Allied forces and their efforts meet with great success and considerable financial rewards.

Signs a contract, prompted by Roberto Rossellini, to co-write the screenplay for the film *Roma città aperta*; his job is to concentrate on the character played by Aldo Fabrizi.

Pages from the *Libro di Mario*, 1944
Cartoons of Camerini, Fellini,
Guasta, and Bompiani, are
represented on the title page
(below left)... *C'erano 4 pittori* ...
(they were 4 painters ...).
The artist friends earned
their keep by drawing comics

and caricatures for the Allied
soldiers at the Funny Face
shops. The book
was a birthday present for Mario,
the son of Domenico Forges
Davanzati, theater impresario
and founder of the five caricature
shops in Rome

A friendship for two generations
With Roberto Rossellini
on the set of *Paisà*, 1945
With Isabella Rossellini
and Martin Scorsese,
her husband at the time,
Rome, 1980

Announcement designed by Fellini,
of the birth
of his and Giulietta's
only child, on March 22, 1945
The child died two weeks later
from a breathing disorder

1945–46

Becomes a father on March 22, 1945. But the only child of Federico Fellini and Giulietta Masina lives less than two weeks and dies on April 1 from a breathing disorder.

Takes part in the first public showing (September 1946) of *Roma città aperta*. This prophetic film meets with wide acclaim.

Contributes to the preparation, screenplay, and production of the film *Paisà*, directed by Roberto Rossellini: their working tour of war-torn Italy and their close friendship are remembered by Fellini as a crucial part of his life.

Pens around twenty installments of his radio show "Le avventure di Cicco e Pallina" (he has changed the name "Cico" to "Cicco"), starring Giulietta Masina, starting in November 1946.

Fellini's comic strip for the weekly
humor magazine, *Il Travaso*
Rome, 1946–47

A page from the comic-strip
'La bimba atomica'
(The Atomic Child)
drawn by Fellini
for the children's weekly
Campanello, 1946

1947
Returns to his work in the film world as a co-writer for the films *Il passatore*, directed by Duilio Coletti; *Il delitto di Giovanni Episcopo*, directed by Alberto Lattuada, starring Aldo Fabrizi; *Senza pietà*, also directed by Lattuada (including Giulietta Masina); *L'ebreo errante*, directed by Goffredo Alessandrini.

1948
Makes his debut screen appearance, with beard and blonde hair, in the part of a tramp believed to be St. Joseph in "Il miracolo," one of the two episodes of the film *L'amore*, directed by Roberto Rossellini, starring Anna Magnani; the other part of the film is Jean Cocteau's one-act monologue entitled *La Voix Humaine* (*The Human Voice*). The concept and screenplay for "Il miracolo" are the work of Fellini and Tullio Pinelli. Also collaborates on the screenplays for *In nome della legge*, directed by Pietro Germi; *Il mulino del Po*, directed by Alberto Lattuada; and *Città dolente*, directed by Mario Bonnard.

1949
Works on the preparation and realization and also co-writes the screenplay for *Francesco giullare di Dio*, directed by Roberto Rossellini. Except for Aldo Fabrizi, the entire cast is non professional.

1950
Co-writes the screenplays for the films *Il cammino della speranza*, directed by Pietro Germi; and *Persiane chiuse*, directed by Luigi Comencini (cast includes Giulietta Masina).

1951
Takes his first trip to Paris.
Works on the film *Europa '51*, directed by Roberto Rossellini, starring Ingrid Bergman. He is co-screenwriter for *La città si difende*, directed by Pietro Germi; *Cameriera bella presenza offresi*, directed by Giorgio Pastina; and *Il brigante di Tacca del Lupo*, directed by Pietro Germi.
Co-directs, with Alberto Lattuada, the film *Luci del varietà* (cast includes Giulietta Masina), produced by a film cooperative.
Directs his first solo film, *Lo sceicco bianco*, starring the comic actor Alberto Sordi, adapted from a story by Michelangelo Antonioni. Also working on the filmscript is the author Ennio Flaiano (who was to provide crucial input for subsequent films, "Le tentazioni del dottor Antonio," *I vitelloni, La strada, Il bidone, Le notti di Cabiria, La dolce vita, 8 1/2, Giulietta degli spiriti*); the music was written by Nino Rota, the composer who left his vital hallmark on all Fellini's film productions.

1952-53
Directs *I vitelloni*, a French co-production; it is his first film to get distributed outside Italy.
Co-writes the screenplay for *Cinque poveri in automobile*, directed by Mario Mattoli, starring Aldo Fabrizi, Eduardo De Filippo, and Walter Chiari.
Wins his first award—the Golden Lion at the Venice Film Festival—for *I vitelloni*. From now on the national and international prizes won by Fellini become so numerous that they will need a room of their own.
Directs the sketch "Un'agenzia matrimoniale."
Directs *La strada*.

1954

Wins the Silver Lion at the Venice Film Festival for *La strada*, a film with universal acclaim that receives over fifty prizes worldwide. Suffers from depression and makes his first foray—through Professor Emilio Servadio—into that psychoanalytic therapy which will have a far-reaching effect on both his life and his work.

1955

Directs *Il bidone*.

1956

Directs *Le notti di Cabiria*; co-writing the dialogues for this film is Pier Paolo Pasolini; in 1959 the film was recast as an American musical (*Sweet Charity*).
Wins an Academy Award for *La strada* (Best Foreign Film); the film's star Giulietta Masina receives enormous worldwide acclaim.
Loses his father Urbano, who dies in Rimini from a heart attack.

1957

Makes his first trip across the Atlantic to the United States to collect the Oscar for *La strada*, and stays over for six weeks at the invitation of Burt Lancaster and the producers, Hetcht–Hill–Lancaster, who would like him to direct a film in America.

Wins his second Academy Award, for *Le notti di Cabiria* (Best Foreign Film).

Co-writes with Tullio Pinelli *Viaggio con Anita*, a film inspired by the death of his father, but never realized (the storyline was later heavily adapted for a film by Mario Monicelli).

Co-writes the screenplay for *Fortunella*, directed by Eduardo De Filippo, starring Giulietta Masina.

1958   Co-writes the screenplay, together with Ennio Flaiano and Tullio
                Pinelli, for *La dolce vita* and begins preparing for the film. At this
                stage he meets Marcello Mastroianni, who is to become his principal
                actor and screen alter ego.

1959   Directs *La dolce vita*.

With his mother Ida
and Marcello Mastroianni
on the set of *La Dolce Vita*, 1959

With Valentina Cortese during
the awarding of the Nastri d'Argento
award, Rome, 1956

With Sophia Loren
at the wheel of her Mercedes
Rome, 1959

Receives catcalls, insults, and protests from the scandalized non paying audience of the preview of *La dolce vita* at the Capitol movie theater in Milan. Owing to its fantastic popularity, the film is suddenly at the hub of a cultural battle of ideas: the opposition to the film includes right-wing political parties who debate the affair in parliament, the church group Azione Cattolica (which demands the film be censored), the General Assembly of Roman Clergy, the geneaological league of the Italian nobility. The left-wing elements of journalism, culture, and politics rally to the film's defense. For months people take sides and discuss little else.

Applies for an audience with the Archbishop of Milan, Monsignor Montini (later Pope Paul VI), in a bid to defend the group of Jesuits who run a cultural center in Milan (Centro San Fedele); after expresing support for the film in their journal, the group was to be severely punished. Fellini's attempt to intervene fails.

Fellini had been more successful in his defense against the censorship of *Le notti di Cabiria* in 1956, with Cardinal Siri, Archbishop of Genoa, a highly influential figure in the Roman church hierarchy.

Wins the Golden Palm at the Cannes Film Festival for *La dolce vita*.

Sets up a film production company, Federiz, in which 50% is held by the producer Rizzoli and the other 50% jointly by Fellini and his manager Clemente Fracassi; the firm's objectives are to produce his own next film and new works by young Italian film-makers. However, the company denies support for Pier Paolo Pasolini's *Accattone*, Vittorio De Seta's *Banditi a Orgosolo*, and Ermanno Olmi's *Il posto*; the firm was featured only in the production of *8 1/2*.

Prompted by the director Vittorio De Seta, Federico goes to see the Jungian analyst Ernst Bernhard at his studio in Rome, a person who is to have an immense influence on his work and personal life. Federico begins a series of regular "psychological dialogues" with Bernhard, on whose advice he begins to jot down his dreams with accompanying sketches; these jottings are made in bound volumes of heavy paper, under the title of "Libri dei sogni." He will keep up these dream annotations for over twenty years, with dwindling frequency, until the regular consumption of sleeping pills to combat his perennial insomnia effectively ends his dreaming activity.

With Anita Ekberg
on the set of *La Dolce Vita*
Rome, 1959

With producer Angelo Rizzoli
(far left) and the president
of the Italian government
Aldo Moro (center), Rome, 1964

With Giulietta Masina
and the Soviet astronaut
Valentina Tereskova
at the Moscow Festival, 1963

1961

Directs "Le tentazioni del dottor Antonio," an anti-censorship episode in the joint work *Boccaccio '70*. Among the screenwriters is the author Goffredo Parise.

1962

Directs *8 1/2*.

1963

Makes his first trip to the Soviet Union to accompany *8 1/2* to the Moscow Film Festival. After much discussion, including the resignation of several members of the jury in reaction to Soviet intransigence, the film is unanimously awarded the first prize. This is the last time one of Fellini's films is entered for an international film competition; from now on they will be out of the running.

1964–65

Wins his third Oscar for the Best Foreign Film with *8 1/2*; another Oscar goes to the costume designer Piero Gherardi, who had culled one already for his contribution to *La dolce vita*. *8 1/2* inspired films by many other directors, including Arthur Penn, Paul Mazursky, Fassbinder, Truffaut, Bob Fosse, Woody Allen, Nanni Moretti, Vadim Abrascitov, Carlos Sorin; it even becomes a stage musical in New York in 1982.

Directs *Giulietta degli spiriti*, his first feature film in color.

Begins to show his interest in the world of magic and strikes up a friendship with the Turin-born Gustavo Adolfo Rol.

Experiments with LSD under medical supervision.

Travels to New York to take part in the American premiere of *Giulietta degli spiriti*, which ends with a party thrown by Jacqueline Kennedy.

Loses a crucial friendship with the death of his indispensable friend Ernest Bernhard on June 29, 1965, in Rome.

Writes the story for *Il viaggio di G. Mastorna*, based on the death of his friend Bernhard; the film is never actually made, but the idea reappears as a comic strip over a quarter of a century later.

Meets the author Dino Buzzati and acts as his guide in a mystery tour of Italy's magicians; Buzzati accepts Fellini's invitation to work on the screenplay of *Il viaggio di G. Mastorna*.

1966–67

Begins preparation on *Il viaggio di G. Mastorna*, a film whose development is fraught with setbacks and disagreements with the producers, coolness on the part of the performers, legal problems, and hurdles of all kinds.

Has a heart attack on April 10, 1967, and spends a month in a clinic for exudative pleurisy, subsequently diagnosed as Sanarelli-Schwarzmann Syndrome, which many held to be a "diplomatic" illness enabling him to drop the *Mastorna* project.

Abandons the *Mastorna* project altogether. His new producer Arturo Grimaldi buys back the film from its original producer Dino De Laurentiis for nearly half a billion lire.

Directs "Toby Dammit," a short episode from the joint film entitled *Tre passi nel delirio*.

1968-69

Directs *Fellini: A Director's Notebook*, an hour-long television special for the U.S. broadcasting giant NBC: an adieu to his project for *Il viaggio di G. Mastorna* and the announcement of a forthcoming film on ancient Rome.

Directs *Fellini Satyricon*, a film that earned considerable acclaim worldwide.

Quits smoking.

1970

Gives up driving.
Directs *I clown* for RAI, the Italian national broadcasting network.
Begins preparing for *Roma*.

374

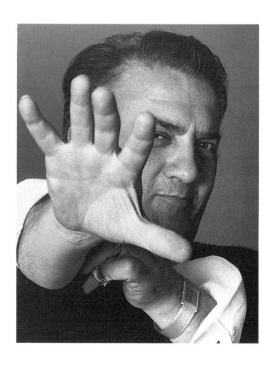

1971	Directs *Roma*.
1972-73	Directs *Amarcord*. Appears as himself in Paul Mazursky's feature film *Alex in Wonderland*.
1974	Receives his fourth Academy Award (Best Foreign Film) for *Amarcord*. Appears as himself in the film *C'eravamo tanto amati*, directed by Ettore Scola.
1975-76	Directs *Il Casanova di Federico Fellini*, a film which was much appreciated only in Japan.
1977	Begins preparing *La città delle donne*.
1978	Directs *Prova d'orchestra*. The film receives its first screening at an "Establishment" gala held at the Palazzo del Quirinale (the presidential residence) in Rome, attended by members of the government. The film galvanized a great deal of debate and many political interpretations.

1979
Grieves deeply at the death of his friend Nino Rota on April 10 in Rome.
Directs *La città delle donne*.

1980
Publishes *Fare un film*, a collection of notes on his work, together with autobiographical material (published by Einaudi).

1981
Begins work on *E la nave va*.

1982-83
Directs *E la nave va*.
His drawings are shown in an important exhibition in Paris, with great success.
Appears as himself in the film *Il tassinaro*, directed by Alberto Sordi.

1984
Directs an advertisement for the Campari aperitif company.
Makes his first trip to Mexico, via Los Angeles, to meet the Peruvian writer and anthropologist Carlos Castaneda, whom he greatly admires.
Death of his mother Ida on September 27, in Rimini.

1985

Directs *Ginger e Fred* in which Giulietta Masina once more stars in one of her husband's films, twenty years after *Giulietta degli spiriti*. Admitted to a clinic with acute circulation problems.

Receives the Golden Lion for a "lifetime's career in film" at the Venice Film Festival.

Attends the preview of *Ginger e Fred* at the Quirinale Palace, once again in the presence of top members of the government and many leading figures from the political and the performing arts world. The official release of *Ginger e Fred* takes place in Paris, marking the first Fellini film debut outside Italy.

1986–87

Publishes *Viaggio a Tulum* in the national daily *Corriere della Sera*, a screenplay in comic strip form of his expedition to see Carlos Castaneda.

Directs *L'intervista*.

Directs a TV commercial for the Italian pasta giant Barilla.

1988	Publishes *Un regista a Cinecittà*, an account of his experiences at the fifty-year-old movie studios where he made nearly all his films (published by Mondadori).
1989	Directs *La voce della luna*.
1990-91	Celebrates his seventieth birthday: the event is commemorated by the movie industry all over the world, by friends and admirers, and by the mass media with a resounding show of affection. Speaks out publicly for the first time with other Italian directors against a law sanctioning the right of private broadcasting networks to interrupt films on television for commercial breaks; their efforts are in vain. Supervises the creation of a comic-strip version of *Viaggio a Tulum*; the artist is Milo Manara. Death of brother Riccardo on March 26, 1991, in Rome.
1992	Directs an advertisement for one of Italy's major banks, the Banca di Roma. Supervises the comic-strip realization of *Il viaggio di G. Mastorna* (the title now carries the addition *detto Fernet*); the artist is again Milo Manara, and the work appears in the monthly magazine *Il Grifo*.

380

Portrait photo taken just before
he won his fifth Academy Award
(for a career in films)
Los Angeles, March 30, 1993

Invitation to
the Fellini's
golden wedding anniversary
identical to that
of fifty years earlier
Their anniversary was on October 30
Fellini died on October 31

1993

Receives his fifth Academy Award, "in recognition of his cinematic accomplishments that have thrilled and entertained worldwide audiences." Alongside him are actors Sophia Loren and Marcello Mastroianni, and Giulietta Masina is in the audience at the awards ceremony in Los Angeles.

Suffers a coronary at the Grand Hotel, Riminy, on August 3.

Dies at the Policlinico hospital, Rome, on October 31. The mortuary chapel is set up in Studio 5 in Cinecittà, while the funeral itself is held at the church of Santa Maria degli Angeli, Rome; thousands of mourners come to pay their last respects.

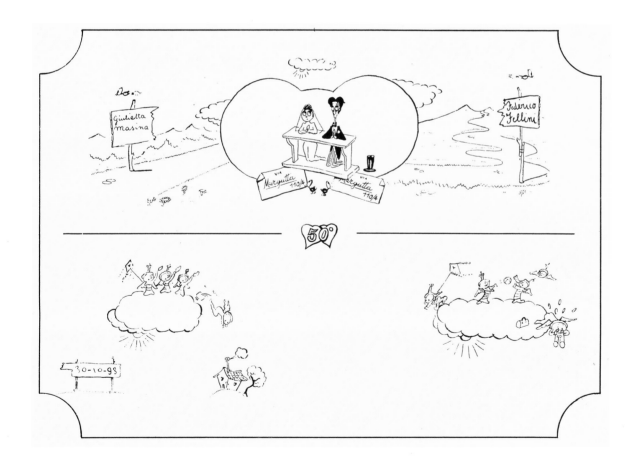

The Drawings

QUANDO ANDAVO A SCUOLA

Quando andavo a scuola ero un ragazzo come ce ne sono tanti: né buono, né cattivo, forse più buono che cattivo, ma pur di risparmiarmi qualche guaio od una sgridata ero capace di fare qualsiasi cosa. A scuola ero un vero disastro ed un giorno il preside mi chiamò: — Ragazzo — disse agitando una mano severamente — così non si va avanti! Ho bisogno di parlare con tuo padre! Domani mattina vieni accompagnato da lui!

■ IL PRESIDE MI CHIAMÒ: "COSÌ NON SI VA AVANTI!"

o tre volte di far un segno al babbo ma egli non mi vide e verso le dieci la mamma m'invitò ad andare a letto. Nel buio della mia camera mi rivoltavo sbuffando sotto le coperte. — Come faccio? Quando glielo dico? — Pensai anche di suonare il campanello e di far salire papà, ma dopo aver allungato la mano verso il bottone elettrico, la ritirai lentamente. — Glielo dirò domattina — e mi addormentai a poco a poco.

All'alba mio padre entrò in came-

■ FUI SUL PUNTO DI DIRE: "PAPÀ, SENTI, C'È UNA COSA..."

Tornai a casa triste ed avvilito.
— Ti senti male? — mi chiese la mamma premurosa.
— No, ho caldo... — risposi pronto e andai a chiudermi in camera mia.
Cominciai a pensare seriamente, a tormentarmi il cervello... Come avrei fatto a dire al babbo una cosa simile? Come sarei entrato in discorso? Quali parole avrei trovato perché egli non si arrabbiasse?
Decisi di aspettare la sera. — A cena glielo dico — promisi ed un pochino sollevato scesi a giocare in giardino.
La sera a tavola, vidi che il babbo era preoccupato e parlava con la mamma di affari che non andavano troppo bene. Quattro o cinque volte fui sul punto di dire — Papà, senti, debbo dirti una cosa... — ma all'ultimissimo momento mi mancava il coraggio e tacevo fissando la tovaglia.
— Non è aria — pensai ad un certo punto udendo papà parlare in tono alto ed adirato con la mamma — glielo dirò prima di andare a letto...
Dieci minuti dopo, mentre la mamma spareccchiava ed io, ormai deciso, mi avvicinavo piano piano a mio padre, il campanello della porta suonò a lungo.
Entrarono sorridenti i vicini del piano di sopra. — Addio — pensai — adesso questi se non è mezzanotte passata non se ne vanno. — e cercai due

ra, tutto vestito e con una valigia in mano. — Sono venuto a salutarti, parto col treno delle sei e dieci, torno questa notte! Fa il bravo, eh? Non far arrabbiare la mamma, studia ed abbi giudizio... — Mi accarezzò la testa e prima che io avessi il tempo di capire e di parlare, aprì la porta ed uscì. Rimasi seduto sul letto stupito e tremante. — E adesso? Il preside? Chi mi accompagnerà? — Udii il portone di casa chiudersi con un grande tonfo ed allora mi appoggiai lentamente con la testa sul cuscino, avvilito e senza sapere che cosa pensare. — Dirlo alla mamma? Confidarsi con lei? Inutile, il preside non vuole le mamme, sono troppo buone, e perdonano sempre... E allora?
Non riuscii a riprendere sonno.
All'ora della scuola, camminavo lentissimo per la strada, con il pacco dei libri sottobraccio. Un passo avanti, un passo indietro... Riprendevo a camminare, mi fermavo, camminavo ancora, trovandomi sempre allo stesso posto.
Ad un certo punto sollevai gli occhi da terra e guardai la strada. — Toh! Ma chi è quello laggiù? Possibile? Sì, sì, era lui, proprio lui, il grasso, rubicondo, il sempre allegro signor Mario!
Con una grande speranza in cuore così avanti e lo chiamai a gran voce alzando le braccia e saltando di gioia:

— Signor Mario, signor Mario, ho bisogno di un gran favore! Sentite, il mio babbo non c'è... Mi doveva accompagnare a scuola questa mattina... ma è partito... Me lo fareste un grandissimo piacere?
Il signor Mario, che conoscevo da tanto tempo, mi guardò sorridendo:
— Ma certo! Figurati... però sento che c'è qualche cosa che non va... di' pure, di che si tratta? — Sapevo che il signor Mario, sempre tanto allegro e sempre così geniale e burlone, non avrebbe potuto ritirarsi. — Sentite, il Preside non ha mai visto mio padre. Vi dispiace di far finta di essere voi il mio babbo? Però vi raccomando... questo è un segreto che deve restare tra noi... — Il signor Mario si grattò il mento pensieroso, trattenendo un sorriso pieno di malizia. — Veramente è una cosa che non sta affatto bene.. Ma se è per farti un piacere, ci vengo!
In due salti fummo al ginnasio. Io, fingendo di essere serio e triste, gongolavo di contentezza. «Questa volta mi va liscia, questa volta mi va liscia...»
Passammo in direzione ed il signor Mario, austero e dignitoso, recitava magnificamente la parte di papà.
— Signor Preside, sono venuto ad

■ ERA PROPRIO LUI: L'ALLEGRO SIGNOR MARIO!...

■ "TIENI, PRENDI!" E GIÙ UNA VALANGA DI SCHIAFFI!

accompagnare questo mio ragazzo...
Il Preside si alzò dalla sedia e salutò: — Avete fatto benissimo, caro signore! Credetemi pure che se non cambia è un vero affaraccio... Condotta pessima!
Il signor Mario ascoltava mordendosi le labbra. — Condotta pessima? Ah sì?
Intanto io per darmi un contegno guardavo una grande fotografia appesa alla parete.
— Ah sì? — ripeté il signor Mario e all'improvviso mi colpì con uno

schiaffone tremendo. A quell'attacco rimasi sbalordito. — Dopo tutti i sacrifici che faccio per te, mi ricompensi in questo modo?
Il signor Mario alzò ancora la mano e mi vibrò un manrovescio spaventoso. Feci un salto indietro, stupito, meravigliato, ansante...
— Ma non lo sai, disgraziato, che mi rovino la salute, in un lavoro che ammazza? E per chi lo faccio? Per me? Di', rispondi, brutto mascalzone che non sei altro!
Di nuovo mi colpì con tre schiaffi rapidissimi.
— Ma alla tua mamma non ci pensi? Non pensi ai sacrifici che fa? Siamo signori noi? A te il pallone, a te le racchette, a te il cinema... Eh! Te lo do io il pallone, te lo do io le racchette, te lo do io il cinema... Tieni, tieni... prendi! — E giù una valanga di schiaffi, e manate sulla testa da far paura...
Con gli occhi fuori dalle orbite, sotto quella grandine, smarrito, stupefatto, senza capire, per un po' resistetti, poi la bocca mi cominciò a tremare, si storse, e cominciai a piangere come una fontana.
Il Preside ebbe pietà di me. Non mi aveva mai visto in quello stato... Veramente quel babbo, sì, era un po' troppo manesco... — Però sono botte sante! — disse. — Botte sante, ma adesso basta... Calmatevi, vi prego! E tu sarai bravo in avanti, vero? Prometti?
Rosso in viso, spettinato, sconvolto, balbettai qualche cosa — Sì... sì...
— E seguitai a singhiozzare in silenzio, mentre il signor Mario prendeva congedo salutando e facendo le sue scuse al preside: — Perdonatemi... ma se non faccio così, questo non mi sente... — Tirando su col naso, salutai anch'io il Preside ed uscii curvo e dolorante dalla stanza.

Quando fummo fuori il signor Mario si aggiustò la cravatta sorridendo: — Beh, che ne dici, te l'ho fatta bene la parte? Sei contento? Un'altra volta...
Con le gote ancora mi scottavano e gli occhi gocciolanti, mi rivolsi di scatto: — Già! Un'altra volta lo dico al mio babbo, va! — e a capo basso, con le spalle curve, e le gambe che mi tremavano di paura e di rabbia, cominciai a salire la scala piano piano...

FEDERICO

preceding pages
Self-caricatures in Africa, 1942

opposite
Page from the children's
weekly *Il Balilla*
story by Fellini illustrated
by Enrico De Seta, 1942

below
Page from the children's weekly
comic *Campanello*
drawings and texts
by Federico Fellini, 1945

Pages from the children's weekly
comic *Campanello*
drawings and texts
by Fellini, 1945 and 1946

Drawings for the typescript
of a film to be entitled
La famiglia (The Family),
1947 (?)

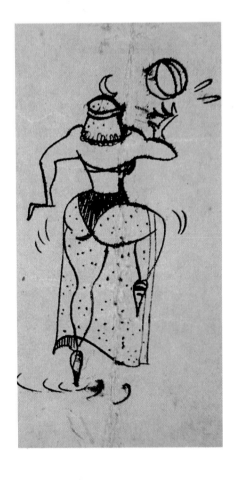

392

394

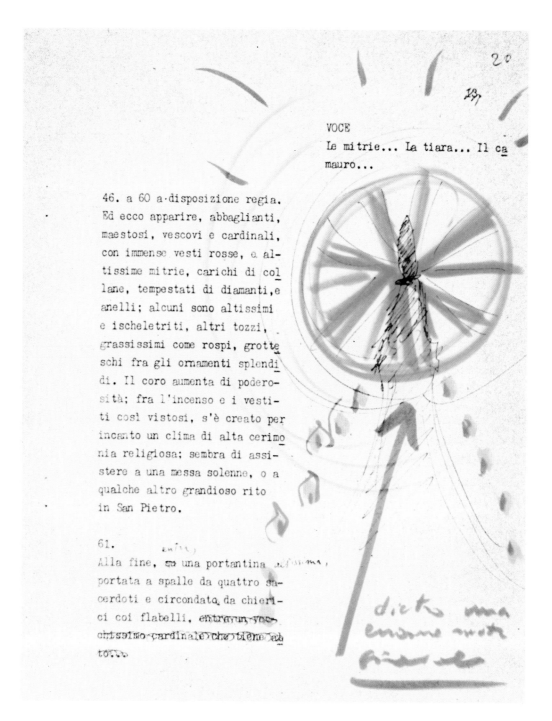

VOCE

Le mitrie... La tiara... Il ca
mauro...

46. a 60 a disposizione regia.
Ed ecco apparire, abbaglianti,
maestosi, vescovi e cardinali,
con immense vesti rosse, e al-
tissime mitrie, carichi di col
lane, tempestati di diamanti, e
anelli; alcuni sono altissimi
e ischeletriti, altri tozzi,
grassissimi come rospi, grotte
schi fra gli ornamenti splendi
di. Il coro aumenta di podero-
sità; fra l'incenso e i vesti-
ti così vistosi, s'è creato per
incanto un clima di alta cerimo
nia religiosa; sembra di assi-
stere a una messa solenne, o a
qualche altro grandioso rito
in San Pietro.

61.
Alla fine, su una portantina
portata a spalle da quattro sa-
cerdoti e circondata da chieri-
ci coi flabelli, entra un vec-
chissimo cardinale che tiene al
torso

The ship *Rex*, from *Amarcord*.

Two drawings for *Casanova*

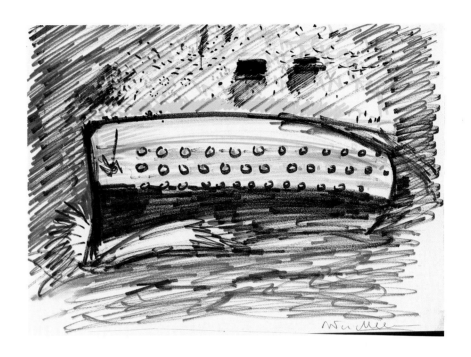

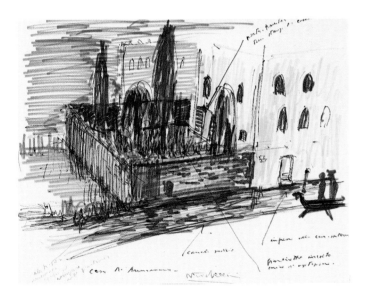

Sketch for an imaginary
advertisement for use in
The Voice of the Moon

Sketches for imaginary
advertisements and the
'super-harvester'
for *The Voice of the Moon*

Federico Fellini
"FARE UN FILM"
dattiloscritto
originale.
Roma Ottobre 1976

Giulietta Masina in *La Strada*
and in *Ginger and Fred*
one of the drawings was used
in Fellini's design
for the cover of his book
Fare un film

410

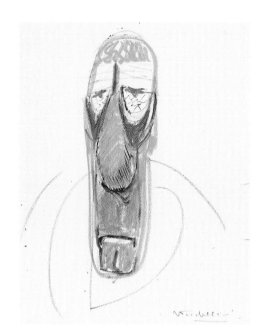

412

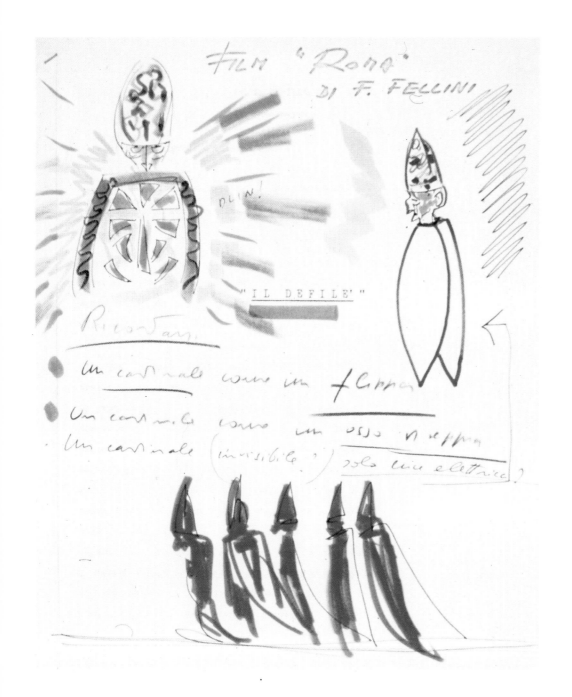

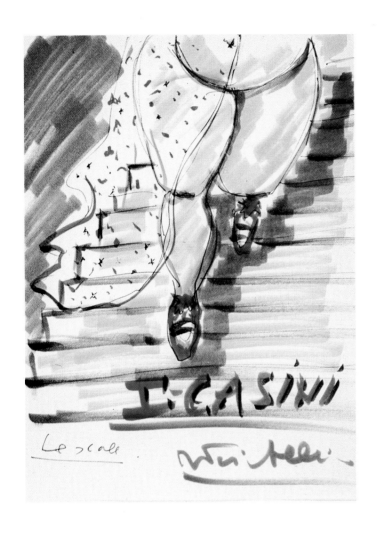

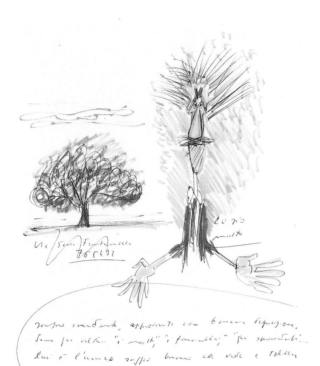

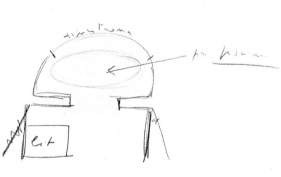

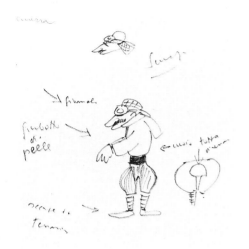

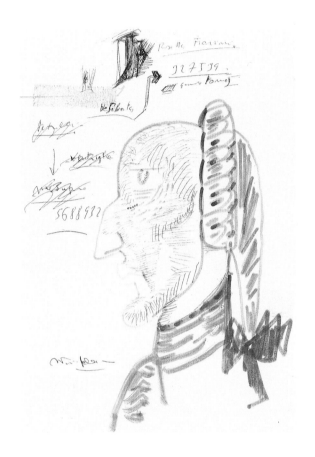

FILM CHARACTERS

Sergio Rubini in *Interview*

Marcello Mastroianni
in *Ginger and Fred*

Paolo Villaggio
in *The Voice of the Moon*

Sergio Leone

Pope Paul VI
deals with a hippy

Giuseppe Rotunno
director of photography

Maurizio Mein, assistant director   Danilo Donato
    set and costume designer

436

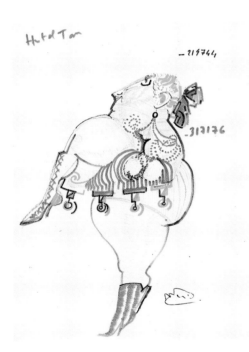

Two portraits of the Moon
for *The Voice of the Moon*

Drawing for a billboard
poster for the set
of *The Voice of the Moon*

Drawing for a billboard
poster for the set
of *The Voice of the Moon*
One of the posters, 1989

"At the beginning of each film
I spend
most of my time at my desk,
and I don't do anything but
scribble tits and ass."

F. Fellini, *Intervista sul cinema*, 1983

Nome : ENNIO
Cognome: FLAJANO .
ETÀ : indefinibile.

DIAGNOSI .

Erotomania acuta. Pericolo a se e agli altri

Inrecurabile.

top
A dream
Signora Carla
Female figure
for *La Dolce Vita*

center
Signora Carla
Saraghina
Saraghina

bottom
Erotic fantasy
Harem woman
Can-can woman

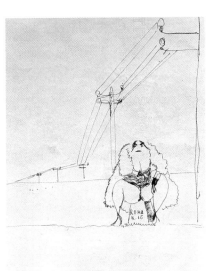
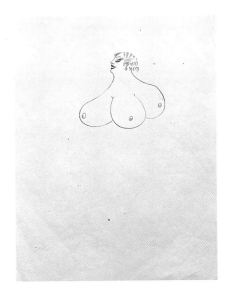

The production secretary
Drawing for *Fortunella*
Saraghina